Life Histories

Socialist History 19

Rivers Oram Press
London, Sydney and New York

Editorial Team
Kevin Morgan
Stephen Woodhams
Willie Thompson
David Parker
Mike Waite
David Morgan
Heather Williams
Julie Johnson

Editorial Advisors
Noreen Branson
Rodney Hilton
Eric Hobsbawm
David Howell
Monty Johnstone
Victor Kiernan
David Marquand
Ben Pimlott
Pat Thane

All editorial enquiries to Kevin Morgan, Department of Government, University of Manchester M13 9PL or Kevin.Morgan@man.ac.uk

Published in 2001
by Rivers Oram Press, an imprint of Rivers Oram Publishers Ltd
144 Hemingford Road, London N1 1DE

Distributed in the USA by
New York University Press, 838 Broadway, New York, NY 10003-4183

Distributed in Australia and New Zealand by
UNIReps, University of New South Wales, Sydney, NSW 2052

Set in Garamond by
NJ Design Associates
and printed in Great Britain by
T.J. International Ltd, Padstow

This edition copyright © 2001 Socialist History Society
The articles are copyright © 2001 Malcolm Chase, Andy Croft, Alison Macleod, Richard Pankhurst

No part of this journal may be produced in any form, except for the quotation of brief passages in criticism, without the written permission of the publishers.
The right of the contributors to be identified as the authors has been asserted by them in accordance with the Copyright, Designs and Patents Act 1988

British Library Cataloguing in Publication Data
A catalogue record for this publication is available from the British Library
ISBN 1 85489 128 6 (hb)
ISBN 1 85489 129 4 (pb)
ISSN 0969 4331

Contents

Editorial	v
Notes on Contributors	viii
Sylvia Pankhurst and the Italian Anti-Fascist Movement The Women's International Matteotti Committee Richard Pankhurst	1
John MacDiarmid's Ghost A tale of socialist Scotland Alison Macleod	29
Extract from 'Letter to Randall Swingler' Andy Croft	40
Mapless in the Wilderness Randall Swingler and 1956 Andy Croft	44
John Saville and the *Dictionary of Labour Biography* Interview by Malcolm Chase	71
Reviews	82
Books to be remembered (2) *British Soldier in India: The letters of Clive Branson* (John Saville)	82
Mary Davis, *Sylvia Pankhurst: A life in radical politics* ((Krista Cowman)	84

J.-P. Sartre (transl. Quentin Hoare), *War Diaries: Notebooks from a phoney war 1939–1940* (David Drake) — **86**

Jeffrey Weeks and Kevin Porter (eds), *Between the Acts: Lives of homosexual men 1885–1967* (Matt Houlbrook) — **88**

Judy Kaplan and Linn Shapiro (eds), *Red Diapers: Growing up in the communist left;* Phil Cohen (ed.), *Children of the Revolution: Communist childhood in Cold War Britain* (Richard Cross) — **91**

Bob Reinalda (ed.), *The International Transportworkers Federation 1914–1945* (Stefan Berger) — **94**

Richard Sakwa, *The Rise and Fall of the Soviet Union 1917–1991* and Stephen J. Lee, *Stalin and the Soviet Union* (Francis King) — **96**

Bernard Davies, *From Voluntarism to the Welfare State: A history of the youth service in England, volume 1, 1939–1979* and *From Thatcherism to New Labour: A history of the youth service in England, volume 2, 1979–1999* (Mike Waite) — **98**

Chris Williams, *Capitalism, Community and Conflict: The South Wales Coalfield 1898–1947* (Alan Sandry) — **101**

Becky Conekin, Frank Mort and Chris Waters (eds), *Moments of Modernity: Reconstructing Britain 1945–1964* (Roger Woods) — **103**

Laura Marcus and Lynda Nead (eds), *The Actuality of Walter Benjamin* (Rosemary Bechler) — **105**

Willie Thompson, *Global Expansion: Britain and its Empire, 1870–1914* (Gita Subrahmanyam) — **111**

Correspondence — **114**

Editorial

Enter any bookshop, and biographies are everywhere: taking up entire bays of their own, infiltrating themselves into other sections and sometimes producing authors—actual living persons—to authenticate their lives. The genre can pander to our worst instincts, and as an approach to history it has been criticised at once for elevating the great and good and descending to the level of personal irrelevancies. 'Is political biography a good thing?', asked a colloquium of the Institute of Contemporary of British History a few years ago, and at least some participants agreed that it wasn't. Nevertheless, for historians of a radical persuasion, life histories provide a sense of agency, context and process often missing from the larger picture. In one of his finest essays, 'Homage to Tom Maguire', Edward Thompson explicitly aimed at recovering this perspective on labour history from that of its 'GHQ' with its leadership intrigues and strategical plans. Modest in scale, it is as good a model in its way as *The Making of the English Working Class*.

Not all biography can be an act of homage, but the different slices of life history collected in this issue each illuminates the seemingly well worn and familiar in unexpected ways. Two of the accounts derive from personal associations. Richard Pankhurst has already published a memoir of his mother Sylvia Pankhurst, a figure who as suffragist, socialist, artist and anti-fascist has exercised a perennial fascination for historians. In his contribution here, he does not draw on his personal recollections, but on a rich cache of papers in his possession documenting Sylvia's tireless work on behalf of Italian anti-fascists in the early 1930s. In the midst of this work she observed that the fate of Mussolini's victims was often overshadowed by the still more barbarous activities of the Hitler regime, and the story recounted here helps provide a useful corrective. It also provides a salutary footnote to the life of another major British socialist, Bernard Shaw, whose attitudes to fascism are documented here to his utter discredit.

If most of us have heard of Pankhurst and Shaw, few will have come across

Alison Macleod's 'great uncle John', the Highland socialist and freethinker, John MacDiarmid. Vividly evoked here, MacDiarmid is a larger-than-life character, dimly remembered from childhood and the subject of colourful family legends. The portrait is a homage of a sort, and also a wistful memoir of the author's own south suburban childhood, when such exotic family connections exercised a powerful attraction. There are always at least two lives in any biography, and one of them is that of its author.

That does not depend on an existing a family connection or personal acquaintance. As Andy Croft indicates in his *Letter to Randall Swingler*, the writing of a biography is itself a sort a human relationship, intimate, or at least transgressing normal rules of privacy, demanding of time and effort, and a means of learning to place oneself as well as one's subject. Lytton Strachey's methods: airily pronouncing without a hint of self-reflection, do not commend themselves to historians of the left. The article on Swingler which follows, describing his break with the CPGB in 1956, shows why for any inquisitive historian, biography is emphatically (in the right hands) a 'good thing'. The emergence of the first New Left has been well chronicled as a turning point in the history of the British left: exactly as the formation of the ILP had been when Thompson wrote his essay on Tom Maguire. Croft provides a chastening version of 1956 as lived experience, which complements and subverts more facile or 'strategical' accounts.

Among the other dissident communists figuring largely in Swingler's story are Thompson himself and his co-founder of the *New Reasoner*, John Saville. Both are names familiar to readers of this journal, and John Saville has frequently been among our contributors. Acknowledging the CP Historians' Group as one of his formative influences, he has consistently held to its conception of a history at once scholarly and engaged and counts as one of the seminal figures in British labour history. Foremost among his achievements is perhaps the *Dictionary of Labour Biography*, a towering work of collective scholarship which gives appropriate recognition to a vast array of labour movement figures, unsung as well as familiar. To mark the appearance of its tenth volume, and the securing of its future under a new editorial team, we include an interview with John Saville by the well-known labour historian Malcolm Chase. This too may be taken as a sort of homage to a magnificent publishing enterprise.

Among our reviews are several which continue the life history theme. Particular mention might be made of the latest in a succession of biographies of Sylvia Pankhurst and the third in a short series of retrospective reviews by John Saville, focusing on the wartime letters from India of the British communist Clive Branson. The recipient of those letters, Noreen Branson is, of course, one of this journal's most valued editorial advisers.

Socialist History Journal

The *Socialist History Journal* explores and assesses the past of the socialist movement and broader processes in relation to it, not only for the sake of historical understanding, but as an input and contribution to the movement's future development. The journal is not exclusive and welcomes argument and debate from all viewpoints.

Other *Socialist History* titles

A Bourgeois Revolution?
Socialist History 1 · 1993
0 7453 08058

What Was Communism? Pt 1
Socialist History 2 · 1993
0 7453 08066

What Was Communism? Pt 2
Socialist History 3 · 1993
0 7453 08074

The Labour Party Since 1945
Socialist History 4 · 1994
0 7453 08082

The Left and Culture
Socialist History 5 · 1994
0 7453 08090

The Personal and the Political
Socialist History 6 · 1994
0 7453 08104

Fighting the Good Fight?
Socialist History 7 · 1995
0 7453 10613

Historiography and the British Marxist Historians
Socialist History 8 · 1995
0 7453 08120

Labour Movements
Socialist History 9 · 1996
0 7453 08139

Revisions?
Socialist History 10 · 1996
0 7453 08147

The Cold War
Socialist History 11 · 1997
0 7453 12411

Nationalism and Communist Party History
Socialist History 12 · 1997
0 7453 12675

Imperialism and Internationalism
Socialist History 13 · 1998
1 85489 107 3

The Future of History
Socialist History 14 · 1998
1 85489 109 X

Visions of the Future
Socialist History 15 · 1999
1 85489 115 4

America and the Left
Socialist History 16 · 1999
1 85489 117 0

International and Comparative Labour History
Socialist History 17 · 1999
1 85489 119 7

Cultures and Politics
Socialist History 18 · 1999
1 85489 123 5

Notes on Contributors

Richard Pankhurst is professor of Ethopian Studies at the Institute of Ethopian Studies, which he founded in Addis Ababa. He is the author of some twenty books on Ethiopa as well as over 200 articles.

Alison Macleod was on the staff of the *Daily Worker* from 1944–57. She is the author of seven books, including four novels and most recently the memoir, *The Death of Uncle Joe* (London, 1977).

Andy Croft teaches poetry in Teeside schools. He has written and broadcast widely on the literary history of the Labour movements, and has recently edited *A Weapon in the Struggle* (London, 1998), a collection of essays on the cultural history of the British Communist Party, and *Selected Poems of Randall Swingler* (Nottingham, 2000).

Malcolm Chase is assistant director of Leeds University's School of Continuing Education. His first publication was an entry in the *Dictionary of Labour Biography* and his most recent is *Early Trade Unionism. Fraternity, skill and the politics of labour* (Aldershot, 2000). He was an editor of *Labour History Review*, 1996–9.

John Saville is professor emeritus at the University of Hull and president of the Oral History Society. In addition to his own writings, he has co-edited three volumes of *Essays in Labour History*, over twenty volumes of the *Socialist Register* and (as described in his interview here) ten volumes of the *Dictionary of Labour Biography*.

Sylvia Pankhurst and the Italian Anti-Fascist Movement
The Women's International Matteotti Committee

Richard Pankhurst

My mother Sylvia Pankhurst (1882–1960) was the daughter of Dr Richard Marsden Pankhurst, a Manchester lawyer and sometime Liberal, who had drafted the first abortive Parliamentary Bill for Women's Suffrage in 1868 and joined the Independent Labour Party (ILP) in 1889. An avowed Republican, who demanded the abolition of the House of Lords and the nationalisation of the mines, he stood, in 1895, as unsuccessful ILP parliamentary candidate for Gorton in Manchester. Five years after his death in 1897, my mother [hereafter Sylvia] won a scholarship to the Royal College of Art in London, whence, in 1902, she gained a year's travelling art scholarship to Venice. There she studied its mosaics, learnt Italian and, of particular relevance to our story, came to know and love the Italian people.[1]

Not long after her return to England, her mother Emmeline (née Goulden) and the latter's daughters, Christabel and Sylvia herself, founded the Women's Social and Political Union (WSPU) in Manchester, and Sylvia became the Union's first honorary secretary in the capital.[2] Ideological differences with the by then largely Conservative WSPU—the Suffragettes as they were popularly known—led by her mother and sister Christabel, subsequently caused Sylvia to move to the East End of London. There, in 1914, she founded the left-oriented East London Federation of the Suffragettes, and edited the *Woman's Dreadnought*, later the *Workers' Dreadnought*. A keen supporter of the Russian Revolution of 1917, she made her way illegally to Petrograd, as it was then called, to attend the First Congress of the Third International.[3]

Sylvia's introduction to fascism seems to have taken place soon afterwards. Travelling to Bologna to meet socialist comrades in 1919 she witnessed fascist *squadristi*, or thugs, beating up the people. This turned her overnight into a passionate anti-fascist. She saw fascism as the antithesis of freedom, workers' rights and the rights of women, and determined to oppose it wholeheartedly. In this she had the support of her Italian companion, my father Silvio Corio, an Italian refugee in London.

The assassination by the fascists of the Italian Socialist Deputy Giacomo Matteotti, on 10 June 1924, had a significant impact even outside Italy. One of its repercussions was the establishment by Sylvia and others of a typically British voluntary society. The history, ideals and activities of the Women's International Matteotti Committee (WIMC), an early anti-fascist organisation, have not hitherto been chronicled. In the course of its short existence, from 1932 to 1935, it organised an influential petition, held public meetings, and despatched letters to statesmen, leaders of opinion, and the press, with a view to drawing public attention to what it considered the iniquities of the Italian fascist regime. The committee also engaged in polemics, notably with the British playwright George Bernard Shaw, and attempted to provide medical facilities for detainees at Ponza, one of Mussolini's penal islands.

Mussolini's militaristic and expansionist ambitions convinced Sylvia that fascist Italy was bent on aggression. Having regarded Italy as the first victim of fascism, she considered Ethiopia, invaded in 1935, to be the second, and subsequently threw herself into another anti-fascist struggle. In 1936 she founded a pro-Ethiopian and anti-fascist newspaper, *New Times and Ethiopia News*. This would eventually take her to Addis Ababa, where she died in 1960.

The first of Sylvia's anti-fascist activities is the focus of the present article, which is based largely on hitherto unused documents in the author's possession.[4]

The beginnings of the WIMC

The WIMC was established in London in the summer of 1932, when it was reported that Matteotti's widow Velia was suffering severe persecution at the hands of the fascist government, and that an Italian physician, Dr Mario Germani, accused of attempting to help her escape from Italy, had been sentenced to ten years' detention on the island of Ponza. One of the first reports of Velia's deplorable position was embodied in a letter from an unimpeachable source: the Italian anti-fascist Carlo Rosselli, then an exile in France, who wrote to Silvio Corio about it on 26 June 1932.[5]

As a result of this message, and others arriving at about the same time, news of Velia's condition reached a handful of politically interested people in Britain. One of them was Sylvia, who was predisposed to take an interest, having witnessed the fascists' emergence in Italy in 1919. She later recalled that clash between the socialists and the fascist assault squads through whom Mussolini and his agents were then working, to William Gillies of the Labour

Party's International Department. 'The Socialists were absolutely blameless, and I ought not to say the Socialists, because the whole people were involved, a great crowd of ordinary citizens.'[6] Sylvia succeeded in interesting three other women in Velia's case, and together they founded the WIMC. As well as Sylvia herself, who became the committee's honorary secretary, these were Charlotte Drake, who had previously worked with her in the East of London; Mrs Patricia French-Barrass, a former miner's wife, and Mrs Helen Allen, who lived in Golders Green, London, and became honorary treasurer until replaced in this post by Mrs French-Barrass.

Other members included three prominent American feminists, Alice Stone Blackwell, Harriett Staunton Blatch, and Rose Scheidermann; the Spanish Deputy, Victoria Kent; the Dutch poetess Roland Holst; the British writers Dora Russell and Ethel Mannin; and the Irish woman Hannah Sheehy Skeffington, whose socialist husband had been murdered, for his pacifist beliefs, in Easter Week 1916.

Ideals and objectives

The committee's political ideals and objectives were stated in an international petition drafted by Sylvia towards the end of 1932. The highly emotive text embodied a sweeping condemnation of Mussolini's regime:

> We…appeal to the conscience of humanity against the cruel persecution of the widowed Velia Matteotti during the 8 years since her husband's murder, a persecution which keeps her and her children under perpetual police surveillance; cuts them off from all intercourse with their kind by punishing with imprisonment or internment all those who dare to visit them; forbids her children to bear their father's name in school or to visit his grave; and imposes on the family a calculated system of intimidations and inhibitions which, as Mrs. Matteotti herself rightly declared, has reduced them to the condition of prisoners, and which has punished by 10 years' imprisonment Dr. Germani who hoped to help them leave Italy. This persecution is directed against a blameless woman, whose only offence is that she is the widow of one who was murdered by the Fascists, because, from his seat in the Italian Parliament, he bravely exposed the iniquities of the Fascist regime.
>
> We are deeply sensible that the persecution of the Matteoti family is but the crowning outrage of a Dictatorship excelling in terrorism and oppression that which prompted the historic protest of Gladstone against the Government of Naples. This Dictatorship has destroyed all the forms

of democratic Government. It has suppressed all newspapers and organisations which are not of its own following. It punishes by sentences of up to 20 years' imprisonment those who belonged to the dissolved organisations before they were declared illegal and has interned on the penal islands, incarcerated in the dungeons, or driven into exile, thousands of the most talented and public spirited citizens of Italy.

The recent amnesty has set free some 35,000 ordinary criminals, but has released only 639 political prisoners, and the vast majority are still incarcerated. Under Fascism, liberated political prisoners, if not immediately re-arrested, pass to a persecution similar to that suffered by the Matteotti family. Unable to work, isolated from their friends, they are menaced by death from starvation. Fascism has expelled women Professors from the Universities and Lyceums of Italy. It compels all University Professors to take an oath of allegiance to the Fascist State; and imposes its official textbooks and propaganda even upon the children in the elementary schools. We register our protest against this appalling and retrograde regime. To remain silent in the face of this outrage is to share responsibility for the deed. We desire to make known the persecution of a defenceless woman and her children. We urge all who cherish ideals of liberty and justice to support our demand that this persecution shall cease, that Mrs. Matteotti and her family shall enjoy the liberties which rightly belong to all citizens and shall be free to reside either in Italy or abroad as they may desire.[7]

A French version was produced by Adrienne Marchand, a musician and member of the French *Ligue des Droits de l'Homme*, who been expelled from Italy in 1928 for befriending Velia Matteotti. In Britain the petition circulated widely in feminist, left-wing, and pacifist circles, and its signatories included Bertrand Russell; Harold and Frida Laski; the Labour politicians George Lansbury, Sommerville Hastings, Ellen Wilkinson and Jennie Lee; the feminists Emmeline Pethick-Lawrence, Charlotte Despard, Dora Montefiore, Evelyn Sharp, and Monica Whately; the pacifist actor and playwright Miles Malleson; and the writers and journalists Naomi Mitchison, Laurence Housman and Henry W. Nevinson.

'Odious persecution'

The committee's position was further formulated in a press statement, also written by Sylvia, circulated both within Britain and internationally. In outlining the WIMC's purpose and objectives, the statement first described the background to Matteotti's murder at the direct instigation of the fascist government:

Matteotti came to this country and arranged for the publication of a book[8] which he had prepared giving detailed information on the huge series of murders and outrages by which Mussolini's administration had secured dictatorial power in Italy. Returning to Rome, Matteotti tabled a parliamentary interpolation dealing with the financial corruption of the Fascist regime, with its methods of violence and with the suppression of the free right of voting, which it had perpetrated in the then recent Parliamentary elections. He delivered a powerful attack on Fascism in the Italian Chamber of Deputies, and a few days later, was kidnapped and murdered, his body being mutilated and hidden.

No less iniquitous was the 'heavy and continuous persecution' of Matteotti's widow:

Her dwelling is under the observation of fifty police agents controlled by an officer of the Fascist Militia. Few dare to visit her. Whoever has the temerity to do so is ordered by the police on duty outside her residence to state his or her name and address, occupation, reason for visiting the unfortunate widow, etc. Even persons visiting people in other flats in the same building are shadowed lest they should slip surreptitiously into Mrs. Matteotti's flat. At night a searchlight plays on her house that all who come and go may be observed.

As well as Germani—sentenced as an accomplice to an act never actually committed—Francesco F. Nitti, the nephew of a former Italian premier and a Liberal in politics, was sentenced to five years' penal servitude when he presented Velia with a wreath for her husband's grave.[9] Even 'the very name Matteotti [was] not permitted in Italy':

The children of the murdered Deputy are not allowed to bear it. They have been denied access to school because their mother refused to send them under another name. Recently, to get some sort of education for her eldest son, she reluctantly agreed to let him be registered at a secondary school under her maiden name. This unfortunate lad is compelled to sing Fascist hymns, to salute, in so-called Roman fashion, the portrait of Mussolini, the man who is charged with direct responsibility for the murder of this young Matteotti's father; the man who to this day dictates the persecution of this young Matteotti's mother!

Formed to bring this 'odious persecution' to an end, the WIMC set itself three main objectives: to make the fact of the persecution known internationally; to 'approach all the Foreign Offices of Europe appealing to them to make representations to the Italian Government'; and to negotiate directly with the Italian government to secure the 'peace and freedom' of Madame Matteotti should she desire to remain in Italy, and the opportunity to leave safely with her children should she not wish to do so. For this last purpose, the statement expressed the committee's objective of an international women's delegation which would to go to Italy 'to investigate all the facts at first hand and deal directly with the Italian Government on Mrs. Matteotti's behalf'.

In accordance with these objectives, in October 1932 the committee issued a penny broadsheet, entitled *Humanity*, which on its front page carried the poignant statement by Matteotti, uttered on the day of his death: 'You can kill me, but you cannot kill the thought within me.' It also approached the British government to make representations to Mussolini, but after consulting with the prime minister, Ramsay MacDonald, the foreign secretary Sir John Simon refused even to see a women's delegation. A letter to the British Embassy in Rome also received a negative response.[10] As Sylvia noted in the letter to US president Franklin Roosevelt, one of a number of international statesmen approached by the committee, representations were needed from more powerful quarters than the exiled free press of the Italians themselves:

> The need for these representations transcends that which animated the historic protest of Gladstone against the cruelties of the Bourbon Government of Naples.
>
> To be silent in face of this crime is to condone it and to share its guilt.

That may seem a fitting comment on the attitude taken by the British government.

The WIMC created some excitement in British left-wing circles. Frida Laski promised the assistance of both herself and her husband Harold Laski, and offered a sobering observation on the basis of their own work for the cause of India. 'English people are inclined to be self-sufficient, and it is hard to get them worked up about people outside their little island', she wrote on 15 July 1932, adding:

> I hope there is more sympathy for Italy than we find for India. If not you must be in the last clutches of despair.

Bertrand Russell, unable to offer immediate financial support, did indicate the possibility of help should the committee struggle to raise funds. From Ireland, Charlotte Despard, the founder a decade earlier of the Women's Freedom League, expressed her indignation at 'the cruelties inflicted by a Monster of Terror on an innocent family' and paid testimony to Sylvia's own 'courage and tenacity' in acting as secretary.[11]

The WIMC also gained support from several societies on the continent of Europe. These included the *Ligue des Droits de l'Homme*, which provided several signatories, and the *Ligue Internationale des Femmes pour la Paix et la Liberté*, both based in Paris. The London-based Italian branch of the former organisation, and the Polish branch of the latter, were particularly supportive. In Madrid, a Spanish branch of the committee was established with Teresa Nevot as its founding secretary. When the Spanish government was approached to ascertain whether the committee's anti-fascist stance would endanger Spanish relations with Italy, the government raised no objection.

Italian anti-fascist reactions

The committee's objectives were welcomed by several leading Italian anti-fascist exiles already acquainted with Velia's plight. These included Carlo Rosselli and the aforementioned Nitti, both of whom had been imprisoned on the penal island of Lipari, but had escaped to France. Gaetano Salvemini and Max Salvadori, former prisoners who had obtained refuge in the US and Britain respectively, also offered their support.[12]

Rosselli was the most dedicated of them. An Italian patriot, whose family had supported Mazzini during the Italian unity struggle, he had engineered the escape from Italy of the veteran socialist leader Fillipo Turati, for which act he was sentenced to ten months' imprisonment.[13] Subsequently he founded Italy's principal non-communist anti-fascist organisation, *Giustizia e Libertà (Justice and Liberty)*. Having initially alerted London friends to Velia's case, Rosselli thereafter entrusted the issue largely to his English wife Marion, *née* Cave, who had herself been imprisoned by the fascists. A committed supporter of the anti-fascist cause, she warned Sylvia that Velia, although 'extremely desirous to leave Italy', had serious financial difficulties, 'which might make it impossible for her to profit by the results of your campaign, should it be successful'. Nevertheless, she offered the WIMC her full support, and on the basis of her own personal experience testified to the efficacy of an agitation in Britain. It was, she said, 'only the campaign in the English press on my behalf which brought about my release when I was arrested after my husband's escape from Lipari, & only the continuation of the campaign which obtained a passport ... an unheard of thing for the wife of an exile'.[14]

Francesco Nitti, now in Paris, also offered his support. Until his arrest, he had frequently visited Velia in the period after her husband's murder and vividly evoked the 'very sad and offensive conditions' she endured with her children under 'the insidious and oppressive surveillance of brutal police-agents'. To draw attention to these conditions, Nitti proposed undertaking a US lecture tour:

> I believe that my personal testimony in a series of lectures in America would be of concrete help to this splendid cause. My book 'Escape', which has had a certain success, has made my name known to Americans and to the readers of several other countries (Germany, Spain, France and Sweden) having been translated in five languages.

In further letters to Sylvia, Nitti described both Mussolini's apprehensions at the possible effectiveness of such international campaigns and the measures he adopted to forestall them. Nitti had not succeeded in obtaining a visa to Britain, and argued that by not delivering passports to political emigrés Mussolini was doing everything possible 'to prevent them of a free circulation in different countries'. He also described the campaign of denials which Mussolini was likely to set on foot, but this itself could be taken as a testimony to the effectiveness of such campaigns:

> I believe that only an energetic and well organised campaign in the principal countries of the World can give the results which we desire to reach to. The fashist [sic] government is fearing mostly, or even only, of what is told abroad about its politics. Mussolini is personally immensely annoyed by every campaign which is done against him or his regime in some foreign countries. I believe that when several and frequent meetings will be organised in the principal foreign cities and when the International press will reproduce echoes of those meetings the fashist government will then understand that the best thing would be to give up.

Salvemini, writing from Yale University, also paid tribute to the effectiveness of a determined few. 'If there were all over the world no more than ten people like you, Fascist propaganda would be hopeless', he wrote on 31 October 1932. Tito Torriano, president of the emigré *Unione Democratica Italiana*, perhaps betrayed less confidence in such campaigns when he proposed smuggling out Velia and her family by either car or aeroplane. He indicated another of the obstacles to the success of Sylvia's campaign when he mentioned the many papers abroad which, as he put it, could 'fall so low, as deliberately [to] put aside horrible crimes, in order to exalt, for money, dreadful criminals'. Mussolini, he concluded unequivocally, was 'nothing else than a criminal and head of criminals'.[15]

Another emigré, Luigi Strurzo, wrote to the WIMC on 1 December 1932 offering his 'earnest wishes' for the 'successful achievement' of its aim.

Dr Germani and the detainees of Ponza

The question of Germani came to the fore in the spring of 1933. The episode was significant in that it showed the extent to which Matteotti's widow was the victim of fascist persecution. He had been detained on Ponza for having befriended her, and allegedly discussing the possibility of her escape. This became known to the WIMC fortuitously on account of the political activities of Max Salvadori, today a far better known Italian anti-fascist. After three years of clandestine activity for *Giustizia e Libertà*, Salvadori had been arrested in July 1932 and sentenced two months later to five years' confinement (subsequently reduced to one). During his detention, he was confined to Ponza, where his mother Giacintha Salvadori succeeded in visiting him.

Giacintha, though living in a country under strict censorship, was aware of the WIMC, though she thought it was called the 'Germani Society'. On returning from Ponza, she wrote a moving letter to Sylvia in which she described having met Germani, who was now a deportee on the island along with her son, and who had provided her with details of conditions on the island:

> He told me that in Ponza, a village of about 6,000 inhabitants, plus 300 deportees and 400 police, there is a great dearth of all medical appliances and especially surgical instruments. The best doctor, a blackshirt militia officer of no great capacity, sends bad cases to Naples by the boat. The crossing, often rough, in the small steamer takes seven hours, during which the patient in need of surgical aid has leisure to die. In these last weeks a village child died of diphtheria, and a woman of appendicitis, for want of the necessary operation.

Her object in writing to Sylvia and the 'Germani Society' was to request that funds be raised for surgical instruments so that Germani, who was often preferred to the local doctor, could give practical assistance to the island's sick.

'I feel certain', she concluded, 'that this act of charity towards those who suffer that their country may again be free, will appeal to all those who bear the flame of liberty in their hearts'. For obvious reasons, she also requested that her anonymity be respected.

The WIMC responded to this remarkable letter by writing to the editor of the *Lancet* and several other British medical publications and organisations, as well as to the *Manchester Guardian*, appealing for support to purchase the surgical equipment Germani needed. The London-based Socialist Medical Association and several private individuals were persuaded to co-operate, but asked precisely what equipment Dr Germani wanted. Sylvia, taking advantage of the fact that the treatment of political detainees was still not fully totalitarian, wrote to the surgeon, care of the British Embassy in Rome, to ascertain his requirements. Germani replied in Italian, appending an English translation which acclaimed the offer as an 'act of Christian charity...above petty human prejudices' and expressed his own dedication to the fulfilment of its humanitarian objects.

News from the island was now brought by Salvadori. After being transferred from detention to house arrest, he had escaped, secretly crossed the frontier into Switzerland, and fled to freedom in England. Almost immediately after his arrival, on 1 November 1933, he wrote to Sylvia to ask how the project to assist his friend Germani was faring. He had had a card from him only a few days previously. But a letter from another friend who had left Ponza only a fortnight before revealed that no medical instruments had reached the island.

Salvadori, the WIMC and Dr. Germani corresponded over the next few months about the surgical equipment. On 5 January 1934 the surgeon informed Corio that, if he received the equipment he needed, he would 'naturally' provide surgical assistance to all detainees free of charge 'without distinction of party'. He felt that such a declaration, also on Sylvia's part, would be important 'to demonstrate to the Communists that we do not want to make it a party issue, but that all must fight together against fascism'.

A few weeks later Salvadori reported to Patricia French-Barrass that conditions on the penal island had been tightened: 'Since the middle of December deportees in Ponza are not allowed to receive any correspondence from people who are not very near relations', he wrote, advising that 'Before sending the instruments it would be better to ask the direction of the confine in Ponza if they allow the instruments to be given to Germani'. Sylvia wrote to the 'Commandante di Ponza' in English and Italian, but received no reply.

This left the committee uneasy and uncertain as to what course of action to follow. Two approaches, as Corio explained to Salvemini at the beginning of February, were under consideration: 'To send [the articles], which risks loss, but with the opportunity of making a public protest if the goods are not delivered; or to draw back, notifying Germani of the impossibility of proceeding'. Corio disliked the second alternative, but asked Salvemini for his opinion.

A further difficulty emerged. In April Salvadori had news that Germani's permission to practice the medical profession had been 'withdrawn'. Hence, as he emphasised to Sylvia, Germani might not be permitted to use the intruments even if allowed to receive them:

> The fact of sending medical instruments has nothing to do with the authorisation of exercising the medical profession. Since the month of December last, deportees are not allowed to receive or send any post to people who are not their very near relatives. On the other hand no doctor can in Italy exercise the medical profession if he is not inscribed in the panel. Germani's name was taken out from the panel when he was sentenced by the Special Tribunal. When he arrived in Ponza, he asked to be allowed to exercise his profession among the deportees and the inhabitants of the island; such authorization was firstly granted to him, then, a few months ago such authorization was withdrawn, probably because the local doctors and the Militia doctor were afraid of his concurrence [sic].

'I think that the best thing to do is to send all the same the medical instruments, as a sign of solidarity', Salvadori concluded. '…eventually they will come back and that would give reason to a strong campaign against the Fascist regime'.[16]

Sylvia, who had written to the Italian Embassy for assurances that Germani would be allowed to receive the instruments, received its evasive reply just days after the news from Salvadori. She replied immediately, and with considerable passion:

> It is known to everybody that parcels may be sent to Italy through the ordinary postal channels.
> What I desire to know is whether Dr. Germani, who is a political internee on the Island of Ponza, may receive, without hindrance, a parcel containing surgical instruments which have been subscribed for by a group of eminent British medical men. As I informed you previously, these instruments have been presented to him that he may use them for

the service of sick people on Ponza, and I am entrusted with the duty of ensuring that he will receive them. I do not desire to enter into the question raised in the second paragraph of your letter, as to whether or not the medical service on the Island of Ponza is, as you say, 'perfectly adequate to the needs of the inhabitants'. I only wish to know whether there is any obstacle to prevent Dr. Germani from giving the benefit of his skill to those who may desire it, without fee. There can be no question that two doctors are often better than one the world over, but of that matter it is not necessary for me to judge.

May I ask you to reply clearly on the two points, as to whether there is anything to prevent Dr. Germani receiving the instruments, and whether, on receipt of them, he will be able to use them.

To this the Embassy's First Secretary replied as evasively as before, 'that there [was] nothing to prevent the sending of parcels to anyone in Italy through the usual postal channels'.

The doubt over whether the parcel would be delivered caused the WIMC to change its policy. The committee decided to despatch the instruments to Germani's wife Elsa, who lived in Trieste. Observing that she had obtained 'from Doctors and other sympathisers' a very complete set of surgical instruments, 'worth more than £40', Sylvia asked Signora Germani if she could write to Ponza and establish whether she had permission to send this equipment to her husband. 'If you get permission, I will send the instruments to you so that you can forward them', Sylvia went on. 'In the meantime, I am writing to the Embassy, stating that English doctors will be offended if their gift is not received as it should be, and I will wait to see what developments arise here.'

Replying in English, Signora Germani expressed a deep appreciation of Sylvia's work on both her own and her husband's behalf. Their plight was an unenviable one.

> My husband must remain still three years and 9 months in Ponza. When the detention expires I really do not know what he will do. All is so difficult for us. The struggle for life is now very hard for everyone and is doubled for us. I can not tell you about the enormous difficulties in our way. I have proved them—and my husband more than I in the last years, each day, each hour. I am working here, teaching German and philosophy, but I do not know how long it will be possible. My little boy (7 years old) is with his father on the island, to keep him company. Also our life is not very easy, we try to make the best of things…

Two weeks later, Elsa wrote enthusiastically to acknowledge safe receipt of the instruments, which she then forwarded to her husband. At first, Germani was indeed allowed to use this equipment, but permission, as Salvadori had anticipated, was almost immediately withdrawn. This, Sylvia wrote to Mrs French-Barrass, 'should have been made the subject of great propaganda, but the trouble is that I have not been able to get the medical profession to take it up as it should. The Socialist Medical Association ought to have made a strong protest, and had the doctors done that, the loss of the instruments would have been recompensed by the propaganda'. On that note, the committee's involvement in the island of Ponza came to a close.[17]

Though the question of providing aid for Dr Germani had come to an end, Sylvia and the WIMC continued to believe their primary task remained to continue rallying international opposition to fascism.

The founding of the WIMC had been followed just a few months later by Hitler's rise to power in Germany in early 1933. Founded to oppose Italian fascism, the committee had thereafter to take account of the existence of a similar regime in Germany. This posed it a major problem in that people in both Britain and France tended to be far more interested in German events than in those in Italy. Many Western socialists and liberals opposed Hitler's dictatorship but were largely oblivious to that of Mussolini. The committee, which opposed both dictatorships equally, felt its duty lay in redressing the balance of public opinion, by emphasising that fascism had begun in Italy, that the Italians had suffered from oppression for over a decade, and that the regime under which they lived should be opposed no less strenuously than that recently established in Germany. The committee therefore continued to put its main emphasis on opposition to fascism in Italy.

Rosselli's visit and an 'International Day of Protest'

Even as the WIMC was pursuing the question of Germani's surgical instruments, it continued with its more general anti-fascist propaganda. In March 1933 it arranged for Carlo Rosselli, visiting England to speak to the Royal Institute of International Affairs, to address a large public meeting at Caxton Hall, Westminster. Writing to Sylvia, Rosselli indicated that he would be especially concerned with the foreign policy of the regime and the Italian internal situation. That summer the WIMC also decided to promote an International Day of Protest in support of the Victims of Italian Fascism. This event was to be held on 28 October, the eleventh anniversary of Mussolini's 'March on Rome'.[18] The objective of emphasising Italian, as opposed to German, fascism, is revealed in a private letter of 2 August 1933, which Sylvia wrote to Alberto Tarchiani, the former editor of the *Corriere della Sera*, and an editor of Carlo Rosselli's refugee newspaper *Giustizia e Libertà*, in Paris. The idea of the day of protest, she wrote, was that money collected could be sent to the committees of the different political parties involved, 'thus ensuring unity in freedom'. Among those she particularly mentioned were the Matteotti Fund of the British Labour Party; the anarchists; the London-based Italian branch of the International League of the Rights of Man; and Giuseppe Emanuele Modigliani, whom she had written to as a friend and as a member of the executive of the Socialist International. Sylvia was particularly desirous of the help of *Giustizia e Libertà* and 'of persons or organisations able to get the news of this event *known in Italy*':

> This is of some importance. If this committee had some money we could be printing thin Manifestini to be sent through the post. My friend Corio used to send a good number of *Becco Giallo* [leaflets] to Commercial addresses in Italy, taken at random from the Italian Directory in envelopes bearing a business name…Would it be possible to get in touch with somebody willing to do the same for this appeal to infuse courage into our friends in Italy?

Within Britain, the object was more particularly to return to the spotlight the victims of Italian fascism, for here 'for the majority of people, and even for Working Class organisations, Fascism only connotes the deeds of Hitler; it even appears that Fascism no longer exists in Italy'.

Sylvia subsequently re-emphasised this point. 'Since the advent to power of Hitler the conditions of the Italian workers have passed very much out of sight and memory,' she wrote to Ani Anzani, chairman of the London-based *Liga Internazionale della Diritti del'Uomo*:

> Our Committee has the advantage over other organisations in that it appears purely humanitarian and, if that is possible, above party; on the other hand it has the disadvantage that it is a very lone organisation with its members… scattered all over the world. It is difficult to obtain immediate financial support from them, although we hope to receive it in due course. Again, many of our members suffer from the common error of the present hour, that is that Fascism is chiefly in Germany. The boycott called against German goods was not called against Italian goods, and yet the situation [in the two countries] was almost the same. I personally see in the anti-Germanism that characterises the wave of anti-fascism in England a danger for peace, as it revives the hatred of Germany, fostered during the war.

> For example our Treasurer has left us, as she says that to combat Fascism in Germany is more urgent than to do something in favour of the sufferers in Italy. In this work of protest in favour of the Victims, which ought to resolve itself in a protest against fascism pure and simple, we should like to unite all persons of anti-fascist views, forgetting for a moment doctrinal differences. Suffering, the prison and deportation does not distinguish between party. We therefore ask that all should unite in this protest, forgetting differences, but money collected in common effort should be sent to those funds that most appeal to the local organisers.[19]

Publicity for the day of protest appeared in a number of British newspapers, and the *Manchester Guardian* gave extensive coverage to a powerful WIMC appeal to the enduring liberal values for which the paper stood. It also sought to deflect possible concerns at its specific focus on Italian fascism:

> Fascism denies and destroys all freedom of thought, party, press, association; exploits and enslaves the workers; tramples on every popular liberty won during the last two centuries; re-establishes the juridical concepts of the Middle Ages; is guilty of the ill-treatment and murder of its political opponents. The Italian political victims, upheld by a high faith in human destiny, have for eleven years resisted unprecedented torture and persecution. Over them lies the agonising sorrow that their families, isolated from friends, surrounded by Fascist hatred, the object of continual menace, daily face the risk of death or violent assault and suffer miserable poverty every day intensified. Their heroic endurance should be made known to all the world.
>
> Our committee does not forget that the German people also lately entered upon the same tragic road. We express our solidarity with their suffering and with every protest made by the civilised world against the newly arisen barbarism. Yet we deem it opportune to issue this appeal for remembrance and support for those who have remained staunch under the same tyranny since 1922.

The appeal was directed to 'every centre of Italian emigration and wherever opponents of fascism are to be found'.

A fortnight before the day of the protest, Sylvia was able to report encouraging levels of support, especially in France. In Paris there was to be a joint demonstration organised by the Italian Socialist Party, supported by the Anti-

Fascist Concentration of all Anti-Fascist Parties, and by the French Socialist Party, while in the south of France ten demonstrations had been organised by the left-wing socialist Pietro Nenni. The appeal had also been published in papers in Switzerland, the US and Spain, and in the Swedish *Social Democraten*, but Britain itself appeared to be 'the weakest in support'. Nationally, the Co-operative Party claimed to have 'too many demonstrations' already in hand, while the ILP had as yet made no promise of support and had only with some difficulty been persuaded to publicise the appeal. Meanwhile, the Labour Party 'took the matter into consideration, and decided that it was very difficult for them to do anything because the November elections took place immediately after the Day, and there is a day for the victims of German Fascism on November 9th. I replied that one cannot help these Anniversaries coming together'.

Naturally, the Italian response was more encouraging.

> The Italian Anti-Fascists publish about fifty papers in different parts of the world, and these have all taken up the Day with enthusiasm. The Italians in this country are the most difficult to work on. They are mostly restaurant keepers... and not disposed to make themselves prominent, or perhaps we should say, those who are in control of such organisations of Italians as exist in London at any rate are mostly in business of some sort. Nevertheless, they have provided stamps for sending out the appeals all over the world, and so will bear sympathy in that way. The Italian Socialist Party, which has its headquarters in Paris, circularised all its branches throughout the world, asking them to work for the Day. Even the Italian Free Masons, Scottish Rite, sent us some stamps.

However, the diversion of attention to Germany continued to pose difficulties. For the *Giustizia e Libertà* group, Alberto Tarchiani observed that 'the anti-hitlerian effort is killing our anti-fascist efforts' when he offered his group's co-operation in this attempt at a countervailing action. From the US, Salvemini was less sanguine, and suggested that even the attention now focused on Hitler might also prove evanescent. 'Within a few years they will get accustomed to Hitler', he wrote gloomily. 'Nobody minds about Italy. Mussolini is there since 12 years. Thus he is right. Mankind is disgusting: *voilà tout*'.

A controversy with GBS

The drafting of the WIMC petition had led meanwhile to a lengthy controversy between Sylvia and George Bernard Shaw. Asked to add his name to the petition, the playwright had flatly refused, claiming that the memorial would only worsen the plight of Matteotti's wife and family. His response to Sylvia was very akin to the correspondence which five years earlier had aroused the indignation of Friedrich Adler and other leading European socialists.

> What the memorialists, including your incorrigible pugnacious self, are doing is making an attack on the Fascist regime in Italy under cover of sympathy with the distressed widow and her orphans. Obviously the effect will be to irritate the Fascists and harden them against their liberal opponents. If you want to soften the Fascist Government, you must accept at least that it is a Government and approach it as a friend, and assuming its desire to be just and humane. Even though you are at a disadvantage of being a foreigner meddling in matters which are Italy's business and not yours, and running the risk of being snubbed accordingly and finding that you had better have left it alone, still if the appeal can be made internationally, and not tarred with any particular brush, and is tactfully worded, it might be worth trying.
>
> But if you do not care a rap, and simply want a handful of mud on the black shirt (where it will not show) then go ahead by all means and pile on the agony, only you must not expect me to sign it, as being a Communist, I am strongly in favour of the Corporate State in Italy as against the Liberal bourgeois democracy represented by the party of Matteotti and Salvemini. Please remember that these virtuously indignant attacks on foreign states have failed to save Sacco and Vanzetti etc etc, and even helped to seal their doom, as I said when I refused to join them. But my protest was in vain; you cannot cure nations—least of all the English Nation—of the vice of lecturing other nations on their moral inferiority. Nor I shall cure you.[20]

In response, Sylvia cited not only the cases of Italians like Salvemini, but Shaw's own earlier assistance in the case of a British conscientious objector, to demonstrate the possible effectiveness of such publicity campaigns:

> When that budding poet, Mr. Eric Chappelow, was stationed outside a barrack yard in little more of his own clothing than his stockings and a blanket strapped around him because he refused to don khaki, I asked your assistance in getting publicity, and I also telephoned to Mr. Lloyd George and had a few straight words with his daughter, Megan, who answered the phone in his stead. The result of our joint efforts was that

Mr. Chappelow was released from his unfortunate situation and thereafter was treated very much better than most of the Conscientious Objectors.[21]

Turning to the committee's idea of despatching a group of women to Italy to demand Velia Matteotti's release, she suggested in more humorous vein that Shaw himself accompany the delegation and take advantage of the country's sunnier climate. More seriously, she rebutted his suggestion that the WIMC appeal was not sufficiently international in scope, and pointed out that the committee included representatives from Britain, France, Spain, Germany, Russia, Austria, America, Holland, Sweden, and Ireland as well as the Italian exiles. She went on:

> I beg to differ from your view that the handful of mud which falls on the black shirt on the account of the persecution of the Matteotti family does not show. I think the fact is exceedingly prejudicial to their reputation and I am fully aware that they know it.
>
> I take exception to your argument about the vice of the English lecturing other nations for the simple reason that I do not recognise nationality at all in this matter. It is a question of ideas and ideals. It has nothing whatsoever to do with nationality. As far as I am concerned, you know, and everyone else knows, that I should be just as eager to do this for Mrs. Matteotti if she happened to be English or if she happened to be a native of Ireland, India, Egypt, or any other nation under British rule. Moreover it is absurd for anyone calling himself a Communist to employ such an argument which is typical, if you will permit me to say, of Liberal bourgeois ideology.
>
> I am sorry to have to tell you that your statement that you are in favour of the Corporate State in Italy is absolutely appalling to me and I must protest that either you are not a Communist, or you do not know how the Corporate State in Italy is constituted.

Describing the structure of the fascist regime in some detail, she dispelled any impression that 'this so-called Corporate State is something on the lines of a Soviet, the community having taken control of the industries, the workers in each industry electing their delegates to manage the Corporate State'. On the contrary, it was nothing of the kind: 'Industry remains in the hands of the Capitalists as it always did', and the government of Italy 'to all intents and purposes is vested in Mussolini and the small cliques of his satellites in the Fascist Party'. The Confederations of Employed persons had nothing of the character of authentic trade unions, and there was 'nothing whatsoever of the character of an industrial organisation in the Government of Italy'. The truth was much starker:

> The idea of the Corporate State was not initiated by Mussolini. It was originated before the dawn of the Christian era; it is simply a euphemistic phrase to indicate that the workers are to remain content in the station of life in which they are born; that their betters are to do the thinking and that they must carry out the toil of the community, as the hands and feet of the human body do the will of the directing brain, without presuming either to express an opinion, or to cherish a desire or an aspiration of their own.
>
> Those who agree with that view of society should call themselves Tories at once and follow the lead of Ramsay MacDonald in putting his neck under the heel of the Tory Party.[22]
>
> I am glad to know that in recent years you have become a Communist but I must say the regime of terror and oppression under Mussolini in Italy seems to me poles apart from Communism. Communism, as I conceive it, entails an equalitarian society in which all shall share the material plenty, leisure and cultural opportunities which modern communities, when efficiently organised, will be able to give their members.
>
> Fascism, as all true Marxists are aware, is a manifestation of Capitalism, which it creates when it finds itself in difficulties, to protect itself against the rising power of the workers and the advance of Communism. Italian Fascism is simply a Capitalist dictatorship, acting through Mussolini and other mercenaries, and differs not at all in essence from the White Terror which crushed the Hungarian Sovietists under the leadership of Horthy.[23] Viewing all this, I have no sense of nationality. I see the Italian situation as one of the phenomena which have developed in this transition period which in a book I am writing now I have called the 'Red Twilight'.[24]

Very aptly, Sylvia reminded Shaw that, were he an Italian, he would himself certainly have figured among Mussolini's victims. Shaw's only response was one of his characteristically snappy little post-cards.

> No; you can't bully me; and you can't even bully Mussolini. If you want to help Mrs. M., and not merely sandbag him with her, you must be scrupulously polite.
>
> Eric Chappelow was not an Italian.
>
> An attack on the Corporate State is, in effect, a defence of the parliamentary system. Both Fascism and Communism can make common cause

against that, up to a point. I know perfectly (human error excepted) what I am about.

Beatrice Webb, one of Shaw's lifelong friends, took a dim view of his admiration for Mussolini, this having been 'fortified…by spending 8 weeks and £600 in a luxurious hotel at Stresa, in continous and flattering interviews with Fascist officials of charming personality and considerable attainments'. She saw in it a personal as well as a political failing, noting 'the absence of any kind of sympathetic appreciation of the agony that the best and wisest Italians are today going through; any appreciation of the mental degradation as implied in the suppression of all liberty of act, of thought and of speech'.[25]

The women's deputation

The WIMC's original petition on the issue of Velia Matteotti's right to leave Italy had included a proposal for a women's deputation to Italy. Each further persecution only strengthened the case for such a campaign. In October 1932 Velia's French friend Adrienne Marchand reported that police had advised Velia to abandon her black clothes of mourning, on the grounds that 'everything was now changed', and that the country 'wanted to forget' Matteotti's death. On another occasion, while outside her own house with her children, she had heard someone cry out, 'They should all be exterminated!'. Though she refused to discard her mourning clothes, it was impossible for Velia to escape such affronts:

> At the sea where she goes in the summer, accompanied by 7 policemen, the boys swim at different times: a policeman is always in the sea at the very same time as they. One day, on the beach, a young student got talking with the elder of the two boys, Giancarlo; he asked him some mathematical questions; the boy answered so correctly that the student cried out, 'Long live Giancarlo Matteotti', and embraced him. The policemen heard. The student was imprisoned for a month.
> Madame Matteotti…placed a cross on the grave of her husband, and some shrubs…Each time she came to bring flowers, she found the cross broken or torn up (she replaced it 8 or 9 times); one day the ground had stones dumped on it, on another day refuse. And each time she put it back in order. Now I understand that the land has been ploughed over like the rest of the field.

When Velia subsequently transferred the remains of her husband to a cemetery, she suffered further harassments and the *carabinieri* prevented the lighting of candles or bringing of flowers. Not surprisingly perhaps, Marchand concluded that it was Velia's wish to leave Italy for either Switzerland or England.[26]

However, Velia herself, who had lived under Fascist persecution for almost a decade, seemed reluctant to incur Mussolini's wrath by appealing for outside help, and had never in fact dared to request a passport with which to leave Italy. Moreover, police surveillance rendered direct contact with her impossible. There was therefore no way of ascertaining how far she would be willing to risk escalating persecution by openly declaring her wish to leave the country, or even whether she would be financially in a position to do so. Uncertainty on this score was intensified when Salvemini wrote to Sylvia with the depressing news that Velia was in a state of 'deep political and moral collapse' and that some friends feared that 'in a moment of discouragement she may write for help to some person in the Government and publish a letter stating that she did not authorise your campaign and does not want to leave Italy'. In such an event, Salvemini proposed that protests be intensified, for only once abroad could Velia be regarded as a free agent: 'Until [i.e. as long as] she is in Italy, her statements are to be regarded as extorted by threat and pressure'.[27]

The committee, though acutely short of funds, persevered meanwhile in its hope of sending a women's deputation as originally planned, perhaps at Easter. Proposed delegates included Hannah Sheehy Skeffington; Katherine Gillett-Gatty, a former suffragette and member of the Women's Freedom League, who travelled widely on the European continent to promote the committee's activities; Simone Téry, the daughter of the founder of the French Socialist newspaper *L'Oeuvre*; Madmoiselle Fournier, of the French Socialist Party; and Teresa Nevot, secretary of the WIMC's Spanish branch. There was also talk of representatives from the United States, Germany, Czechoslovakia, Switzerland, Holland, Denmark, Norway, and Sweden.

Even within the committee, however, there was an awareness of obstacles to the success of such a broadly political, as opposed to a purely humanitarian, campaign. Téry noted, from a French perspective, that 'Everything has been said here against the fascist regime, and just now there is a marked tendency in government circles as well as journalistic for a friendship between Italy and France'. For that reason the moment seemed in her opinion 'ill chosen' for an anti-fascist campaign, whereas 'a "delegation" that would negotiate for the sake of a person without seeming to interfere in the interior politics of Italy might have success'.[28]

In fact events in Italy, doubtless in response to the committee's agitation, unfolded in such as way as to prevent this next stage in the campaign from being put to the test. In February 1933 Mrs Gillett-Gatty reported that the widow's house was less strictly supervised than previously, and by July it emerged that Velia was at long last allowed to receive visitors, while her sons were permitted to use their father's name. Germani, meanwhile, was prematurely released from Ponza.

Two months later, Salvemini wrote to Sylvia that he was 'sorry' to say that 'according to quite reliable information Signora Matteotti, finding herself in very difficult circumstances, accepted the help of Mussolini in lending money from a bank. We must be indulgent', he added, 'towards that unhappy and lonely woman. But it is so disgusting!' What had happened, as Sylvia discovered, was that Velia and her children had 'come under the protection of the Catholic Church'. The widow's long years of persecution had thus come to an end at last. The WIMC, which had been founded to secure Velia's release, had thus achieved its immediate aim. The committee was, however, to continue to exist for almost two more years.[29]

Sylvia and another former suffragette, Hannah Laurie, then joined with a French woman Madame Duchesne, and several others, both socialists and communists, in founding a new organisation called the Women's Committee against War and Fascism.[30] Laurie served as secretary and Sylvia as treasurer, the latter in the express hope of 'getting hold of women', particularly those who had been in the 'old Suffrage and Suffragette Movements', but were 'not actually in the Labour Movement', and probably would 'not join anything except a women's society'.[31] Though outside the scope of the present article, this committee may in a sense be regarded as a continuation of the old WIMC, without the latter's commitment to Velia Matteotti.

Shaw once more

Sylvia's controversy with Shaw was resumed in 1935. The ensuing correspondence reveals clearly how Sylvia and the WIMC were concerned with much wider issues than the murder of Matteotti and the persecution of his family. On learning, to her great surprise, that Shaw had accepted membership of an International Committee of Writers against Fascism, Sylvia wrote immediately to remind him of his definite approval of fascism in a correspondence with her stretching as far back as 1928. Did this, she wondered, signify Shaw's belated understanding that fascism was 'a totally reactionary movement...destructive of all the causes with which you have sided during a long and useful life'? In view of his record, *Giustizia e Libertà*, still edited by Rosselli, had raised objections to Shaw's nomination to the committee, pointing out that he had consistently eulogised the dictators and failed to offer his support for their victims. Sylvia too could not help reflecting on so dramatic a change of front:

> When Hitler rose to power, and the Nazis visited their terror on Jews, Socialists and all Pacifists and Reformers, and particularly against the writers and thinkers of Germany, I pleaded with you that, at last, you would declare against this evil and reactionary movement, and at least raise your voice to defend the German intellectuals, even if you felt no solidarity with the Socialists and Communists.
>
> Well, better late than never; I rejoice that at last you have decided to separate yourself from the Fascism reaction, and have seen through the phantasmagoric Corporate State, the hughest sham ever offered to a credulous world!

Perhaps, she reasoned, the explanation of his change of heart lay in the threatening international situation in which 'a powerful bloc of Fascist and pro-Fascist Governments' seemed to threaten 'a life and death contest between the forces of privilege and reaction, and those of Freedom and progress'. She noted that there were 'active and powerful influences' within Britain who wished to draw it into the 'reactionary Fascist group', and cited as evidence the Anglo-German Naval Agreement of 1935 and the assistance quietly provided by the National Government for Mussolini's attack on Abyssinia. 'I cannot doubt that you are alive to these tendencies, and that they have aroused you to signify your change of opinion in regard to Fascism', she concluded. 'I await the vigorous exposure of the sinister character of Fascism, which I trust you now intend.' She signed herself off, 'Your fellow Socialist, Sylvia Pankhurst'.

Alas, it was all a misunderstanding. Shaw had by no means changed his stand, and had accepted nomination to the writers' committee without realising its anti-fascist character. The response he now made to Sylvia included a lengthy theoretical analysis which bordered on special pleading:

> As against Salvemini, Rosselli, and the Liberal parliamentarians, generally I am on the side of Mussolini. Liberty, as understood by his opponents, is, as he said, a putrefying corpse; and he interpreted mass feeling correctly when he assumed that people were sick of endless cackle about capitalist 'freedom', and wanted discipline, organization, silence, authority, and national consciousness. His Corporate State is an immense advance on

Laisser faire. His difficulty is that a Corporate State which is not also a Communist State, owning all the sources of production it has to control, is only a scrap of paper and an explosion of gas. But he is a long step nearer to learning this than his Liberal opponents.

All revolutionary leaders have thus to organize a revolutionary police. Such a police begins without traditions of public service and responsibility, and almost without discipline. It is joined not only by enthusiastic young idealists and hero worshippers, but by Sadists and gangsters who murder, torture, levy blackmail, and gratify their personal hatreds and lusts whenever they get the chance until the new order is established and they can be weeded out ruthlessly.

Meanwhile the inevitable outrages they commit are seized upon by the reaction to prove that the revolutionists are villains of the very darkest hue. All the political incapables who can grasp nothing bigger than a sensational police case become shrieking deserters. The big issue of Liberal party parliamentarians versus Fascism shrinks into *THE MURDER OF MATTEOTTI*. And when the murder of Matteotti leaves me as unmoved politically as the liquidation of the Tsar, you write and tell me that I have changed my opinions, which is exactly what I have not done. If I changed my opinions at every assassination I should have no opinions at all.

Give your mind seriously to this, Sylvia; for you are much given to shrieking. For instance, you never approach me except to shriek at me.

Don't.

Sylvia's response was immediate, and the reader may be left to judge who was shrieking.

You say the murder of Matteotti leaves you 'unmoved', but Matteotti was murdered because he was engaged in exposing the patent fact that Fascism had come to break the Socialist Movement, and to develop the most reactionary type of capitalism ever known. It is because Matteotti had the courage to stand up and tell the truth, where others refrained to save their lives, that many, even of the bourgeoisie, who lacked his courage and did not share his convictions, honour his memory today.

You say that Mussolini is a long chalk nearer to learning the futility of his Corporate State from his experience than are his liberal supporters, but, of course, Mussolini was brought up in the Socialist Movement, which was, theoretically, better informed in Italy than ever the Socialist Movement has been in this country. He had heard the theories of Marx expounded time and time again by men who have studied his doctrine seriously, not by the sort who have only read a pamphlet about him, or perhaps not even that, who call themselves Marxists in this country. Moreover, he sprang from the working class, not from the ranks of déclassé intellectuals and down-at-heel bourgeoisie and he knew perfectly well what he was about when he placed the shackles of Fascism on his fellow workers. To him it was merely a matter of self-interest. His doctrine may be confused, but not so confused that he ever thought there was any salvation for the masses through Fascism!

You have said that liberty, as understood by the upholders of Capitalism, is a 'putrefying corpse'. To a large extent you are right, for if people are the slaves of economic stress, as so many are everywhere today, they often find themselves unable to exercise the liberty of standing up for their convictions as they would desire, but at least, in the non-Fascist countries, most of us are able to do propaganda for our convictions, as you and I do. Your whole life is devoted to propaganda; if you lived in Italy, you would not be permitted to do any propaganda, except on behalf of the ruling clique, and the big interests which keep them in power. You would not be permitted to say that the Corporate State is a 'scrap of paper and an explosion of gas'. There are men and women in the dungeons and on the penal islands of Italy for saying just that very thing, and I warrant if you say it long enough, you will not be permitted to go to Italy for your holidays, as you are in the habit of doing, nor will your plays any longer be permitted there. Dare to write about it in the 'Times', and this will be the result.

Shaw, meanwhile, having learned that the writers' movement stood for 'culture against war and Fascism', promptly refused any further association with it.

The invasion of Ethiopia

The Italian fascist invasion of Ethiopia, on 3 October 1935, moved public opinion throughout Britain and the democratic world. It also met with an immediate response from the WIMC. Within four days the committee had launched a fund to assist the victims of the aggression, which was characterised by extensive aerial bombing of civilians. The committee also wrote shortly afterwards to the Secretary-General of the League of Nations, Joseph Avenol, appealing for his support for Italian soldiers opposed to serving in the invasion. Avenol, who had adopted a pro-fascist line, does not appear to have answered.

Increasingly, however, the committee turned its attention from Italy to

Ethiopia. Sylvia urged that assistance be sent to the Ethiopian Fund of Mercy, organised by the Ethiopian Minister in London, Dr Charles Workneh Martin. The committee also joined the widespread opposition to the Hoare-Laval Plan of December 1935. This was generally regarded as a surrender to Mussolini, because it would have granted the invader large stretches of Ethiopian territory.[32] On 13 December Sylvia wrote at length to the British prime minister, Stanley Baldwin, on the WIMC's behalf, reminding him that the proposed terms of settlement flagrantly violated the Covenant of the League of Nations and ran counter to the spirit of the British people as manifested in the year's Peace Ballot.[33] She also claimed that Baldwin's recent election victory had depended on the appearance of support for sanctions, and that should these now be abandoned the mass of British people would regard it as a 'sacrifice of principle…to save fascism, which does not represent the will of the Italian people, but is a military dictatorship maintained by force of arms and the suppression of democratic institutions'.

The WIMC's overtly political approach to assistance for Ethiopia was not appreciated across the board. Early the following year another voluntary society in Britain, the Abyssinia Committee, proposed to establish an Abyssinia Association to mobilise public opinion on the victim nation's behalf. Sylvia suggested that Modigliani, the Italian representative to the Labour and Socialist International, be invited to address a public meeting in opposition to the aggression on his forthcoming visit to Britain. However, this offer of support was not accepted by the Abyssinia Committee. Its secretary, professor Stanley Jevons, was frightened of taking an anti-fascist stance, and thus becoming involved in what he dismissed as 'politics'. He accordingly replied to Sylvia that its committee had decided unanimously that it 'did not wish to be associated in the public eye with an anti-Fascist organization …[and] feel that linking the question of protest against the War and assistance to Abyssinia with condemnation of Fascism is impolitic'. Sylvia, inevitably, rejected such a view: 'After all, it is Fascism which is making war in Abyssinia, and no-one else'.

The WIMC's participation, with women's, peace, Labour, anti-fascist, and Africanist organisations, in a great Trafalgar Square demonstration in support of Ethiopia and the League of Nations on 17 May 1936 turned out to be the committee's swansong. Indeed, it no longer had a role. For although its ideals, as exemplified in much of Sylvia's correspondence, were general and political, its avowed aims had been quite specific. Velia's persecution, largely as a result of the Committee's agitation, had at last come to an end. Germani had been released from Ponza, and the flow of refugees from fascist Italy was beginning to decline.

In the changed political climate Ethiopia, victim of fascist aggression, provided a new and sharper focus for many if not most of the Committee's members. Symbolic of this change was the fact that within little more than half a year of the opening of hostilities, Sylvia Pankhurst, the editor of *Humanity*, had founded an entirely new publication, *New Times and Ethiopia News*, in the African country's defence.

Notes

1. For an account of her artistic studies and later life, see Richard Pankhurst, *Sylvia Pankhurst. Artist and crusader* (New York and London, 1979); and Ian Bullock and Richard Pankhurst, *Sylvia Pankhurst. From artist to anti-fascist* (London, 1992).
2. For her own evaluation of Sylvia Pankhurst's family background, see E. Sylvia Pankhurst, *The Suffragette Movement. An intimate account of persons and ideals* (London, 1931).
3. For Sylvia Pankhurst's work in the East End, and her socialism, see her books *The Home Front* (London, 1932) and *Soviet Russia as I Saw It* (London, 1921); also the unpublished text of her *In the Red Twilight*, on deposit in the International Institute for Social History, Amsterdam (hereafter IISH); also Mary Davis, *Sylvia Pankhurst. A life in radical politics* (London, 1999).
4. These are currently still uncatalogued, but can be identified by author, addressee and date.
5. For Corio see *Dizionario Biografico degli Italiani*, vol. 24 (1983) pp.87–90.
6. S. Pankhurst to W. Gillies, 9 January 1936.
7. A further statement on 'The Matteotti Case' is preserved in the Pankhurst Papers, IISH, no.289.
8. Giacomo Matteotti, *The Fascists Exposed* (London, 1924).
9. F.F. Nitti, *Escape. The political narrative of a political prisoner* (London, 1930).
10. Correspondence listed in Foreign Office index (Public Record Office, London) but destroyed.
11. Letters to Sylvia Pankhurst from F. Laski, 15 July 1932, B. Russell, 2 December 1932 and Charlotte Despard, 7 February 1933.
12. On his stay on Ponza, the 600 guards there, and the medical conditions confronting Dr Germani, see Massimo Salvadori, *Resistenza ed azione (ricordi di un liberale)* (Foggia, n.d.), pp.107–10, and J. and E. Lussu, *Alba Rossa transeuropa* (Ancona, 1991), p.17.
13. For Rosselli see G. Salvemini, *Carlo and Nello Rosselli* (London, 1937) and A. Garosci, *La vita di Carlo Rosselli* (Rome, 1945).
14. M. Rosselli to Sylvia Pankhurst, 3 August 1932. On Marion's arrest, and the British agitation for her release, see Garosci, *La vita*, vol. I, p.111, vol. II, p.135.
15. Nitti to Sylvia, 22 September, 9 October and 30 October 1932; Salvemini to Sylvia, 7 August and 31 October 1932; Torriano to Sylvia, 27 August and 10 December 1932.

16. Pankhurst Papers, IISH, no.315; Salvadori to Sylvia 11 and 16 April 1934.
17. Sylvia gave a detailed report on this in a letter to the *Manchester Guardian* of 20 February 1935.
18. Advance information on this Protest Day appeared for example in the *Manchester Guardian* of 22 September 1933.
19. On the life of Anzani, and his tragic death on the 'Arandora Star', see *New Times and Ethiopia News*, 20 July 1940.
20. The case of two American anarchists of Italian origin, Nicola Sacco and Bartolomeo Vanzetti, executed in 1927, after being convicted of murder on flimsy evidence six years earlier.
21. This incident is described in Pankhurst, *Home Front*, pp.316–317.
22. Ramsay MacDonald, leader of the then pro-Conservative, or Tory, National Government.
23. The pro-fascist Hungarian dictator Miklòs Horthy de Nagybanya.
24. Drafts of this projected history of the post-First World War socialist movement are preserved in the Pankhurst Papers, IISH, nos.76–80, 83, 86–8.
25. Margaret Cole (ed.), Beatrice Webb's *Diaries 1924-1932* (London, 1956), p.155.
26. Marchand to S. Pankhurst, 4 October and 29 November 1932.
27. Salvemini to S. Pankhurst, 11 October 1932.
28. Téry to S. Pankhurst, 15 December 1932
29. Gillett-Gatty to S. Pankhurst, 3 February and 10 July 1933; Salvemini to Pankhurst, 12 September 1933; Pankhurst to Adrienne Marchand, 10 December 1934.
30. A file on this organisation is to be found among the Pankhurst Papers, IISH, nos.291–3.
31. Sylvia to W. Gillies, 9 January 1936.
32. See D. Whaley, *British Public Opinion and the Abyssinian War 1935-6* (London, 1975).
33. The 'Peace Ballot', or to use its official name, the National Declaration on the League of Nations and Armaments was an unofficial poll, organised in Britain, in the summer of 1935, by the League of Nations Union. Over eleven million answered questions, a little more than half as many as voted in the subsequent General Election of November 1935. In the ballot over ten million people declared that members of the League of Nations should combine to resist aggression. F. Hardie, *The Abyssinian Crisis* (London, 1974), pp.51–2.

John MacDiarmid's Ghost
A tale of socialist Scotland

Alison Macleod

The future of Scotland was clear to great-uncle John. It was a socialist future, free from capitalists, landlords, whisky, tobacco and deer forests. (These are not forests in the English meaning, but bare tracts of country left uncultivated for the chase.) Only as the author of a pamphlet *The Deer Forests, and How They are Bleeding Scotland White*, do even specialised historians remember the name of John MacDiarmid.

I remember him as an upright, alert old man, who liked to dress up in a kilt to go visiting. He drew my attention to the touch of authenticity—a dirk hidden in one stocking. The year was 1930; he was 75 and I was ten. My father, born and bred in Edinburgh, had brought me there for the first time. Everything about Scotland seemed to me wildly romantic. The way of speech was foreign enough to be exciting. Distant cousins greeted us with cries of welcome: 'Come ben the hoose, come ben!' An insufficiently distant cousin practised the bagpipes in a small room.

Cousin Daisy, in whose honour John put on the kilt, was famous for her teas. The spread before us was indeed magnificent, and I could scarcely wait. I was a greedy little girl. However, it was unthinkable in Scotland to sit down to the table without first saying grace. John said sarcastically to my daddy: 'You say grace! Your feyther was an elder of the kirk.' 'Now, John!' exclaimed Cousin Daisy, suddenly agitated. I did not understand either John's mocking tone or Daisy's reproof. It had been kept from me that John was a militant atheist, likely at any time to turn up at a relation's house declaring: 'When we were children we were told that if we weren't good we would go to Hell. Lies, all lies!'

John's younger brother, great-uncle Jimmie, rivalled John in my affections because he had a tramcar in his garden. It would have been in keeping with Highland traditions if he had gone out in the night and lifted it. But in fact he had bought it from the proper authorities. Jimmie said it made an ideal greenhouse. He was proud of his flowers, but for me the most beautiful thing about the garden was the view of the Pentlands. A child of southern England, I envied the people of Edinburgh, who could look from their gardens at wild moors. I envied the children running barefoot in the Old Town. Why couldn't I go barefoot? Life was more fun without shoes.

Old women used to meet for a gossip in the Grassmarket. I saw them sitting on the steps, wearing the long skirts of an earlier age, their black shawls wrapped close round them even in the sunny weather. They were smoking smelly clay pipes. I could not understand one word they were saying to each other. I could not even guess at their thoughts. When I made up stories, they were about brigands in Andalusia. I thought I was quite capable of entering into the brigands' minds. Then why was I baffled by the minds of these women before my eyes?

It was great-uncle John who told me what their lives had been like. When canvassing for the Labour Party, he had explored all the wynds of the Old Town. 'The water's on the ground floor,' he explained. 'So a woman may have to carry it up ten stories.'

Not that John considered the women's hard lives an excuse for their clay pipes. He was ahead of his time in thinking of tobacco as a poison, scarcely less dangerous than alcohol. And he refused to regard the workers as mere victims, who could not help their bad habits. His kind of socialism demanded of the workers that they should exert their own free will, cast aside these addictions and rise up as human beings.

Walking near the Forth Bridge, John talked about his adolescent experience of alcoholism. At his father's fish shop one of the women customers used to look at him and say: 'If I'd had a laddie like yon, he'd have kept me straight.' One day a gale caught her shawl and tore it open, showing that she was naked above the waist. She had pawned her clothes to buy drink. 'It was a beautiful body,' added great-uncle John.

Farming, fishmongering and family secrets

John's father had not always been an Edinburgh fishmonger. Before that Duncan MacDiarmid had been a farmer on the Isle of Mull. Still a bachelor in his forties, he was visited one afternoon by Mrs Mackinnon, the wife of a neighbouring farmer, who was collecting for the kirk. With her came her 12-year-old daughter, Jessie. Duncan apologised for not being able to offer them tea. It was his housekeeper's afternoon off. Mrs Mackinnon said: 'Show Jessie where you keep things; she'll make the tea.' Jessie, with astonishing speed, produced a substantial meal. As they tucked in Mrs Mackinnon said: 'But you should have a wife!' Duncan replied: 'I think I'll just wait for Jessie.'

He waited for Jessie. When she grew up they were married and lived happily...or so I was told as a child. But later an immensely old lady told me what she had heard from her grannie. Jessie Mackinnon cried all night before the wedding, because her parents were making her marry this old man. The year was 1848; the groom was 48 and the bride barely 18.

Jessie, before she was 37, had ten children. They all learned to read and write in English, but they spoke Gaelic too. The first three children were girls; John was not born until 1855. By the time the boy reached his teens, Duncan was feeling the inconvenience of having married so late in life. His strength began to fail before he had a son old enough to take over the farm. So in 1870 the family moved to Edinburgh. Such were the rigours of a farmer's life on Mull that fishmongering seems to have been a cushy retirement job. On the proceeds, Duncan fed and educated his family.

He was even able to make an occasional loan to an old friend, Charlie Macnab. Like Duncan, Charlie came originally from Glenlyon in Perthshire. They had played together as boys. So Duncan, a sober man, was willing to overlook his friend's fondness for whisky. But one evening Charlie came to ask for a loan when he had obviously had too much already. Duncan's patience snapped. He said it was a disgrace that an old man—a retired schoolmaster, too!—should give such a bad example to the young.

Charlie was drunk enough to be eloquent. He said: 'Duncan MacDiarmid, Charlie Macnab has his faults and failings, but so has every man who ever walked this earth save One.' He looked devoutly upwards. 'But Charlie Macnab can lay his hand on his heart and say that he comes of decent people. Duncan MacDiarmid, the blood of the worst man that ever auld Scotland bred runs strong in your veins. You don't want your wife to know it; you don't want your son to know it; but you know and I know that you're descended from Captain Campbell of Glenlyon!' He made a dramatic exit.

Young John, enthralled, asked his father—were they descended from the officer who, in 1692, carried out the massacre of Glencoe? Duncan denied it. A few days later Charlie Nacnab came round, sober, to apologise. He and Duncan were friends again, and the matter appeared to be closed.

Duncan lived until 1883. By that time John's younger brother, Jimmie, was running the fish business. It never made him rich, but it paid for the garden (with tramcar) which I saw in 1930. John, who was by far the brainier, went into the Audit Office of the North British Railway and became an accountant.

There were no such opportunities for his sisters. One of them, Flora, had already spent a year keeping house for her mother's bachelor brother, Hector Mackinnon, a Highland farmer. The arrangement was that at the end of the year she should have £5 and a calf. Nothing in the work of the farm or farmhouse surprised Flora. What did surprise her was that, from the £5, her uncle deducted the amount it had cost him to feed the calf.

In Edinburgh she discovered a career which, even in the 1870s, was open to women. She began to train as a Presbyterian missionary to China. Many years later, her son went walking where Hector Mackinnon had lived, and found old people who remembered him. They said that, after he retired from farming, he walked five miles every day to the nearest railway station. There, he sat and read the stationmaster's copy of *The Scotsman*. Then he walked the five miles back. The neighbours approved of this thrifty habit. They regarded him, they said, as the best type of Highland gentleman.

Neither whisky nor the kirk

In a country where misers were admired, young John liked to pose as a miser. This probably saved him from a great deal of unwanted conviviality. His refusal to smoke or drink must have bewildered his colleagues. There was a strong temperance movement in Edinburgh, but it was almost entirely religious. John's atheism put him outside any accepted category. Besides, it scandalised his relations. The whole family was imbued with the stern religion which Flora was planning to export to China.

A Scot who denounces both whisky and the kirk is making enemies enough, but John contrived to make more. As an accountant, he analysed the Railway Superannuation Scheme, which was administered by some of his superiors. It was financially unsound, he said—loudly, and in public. It was hinted to him that his agitation for change might prejudice his career. The only effect of these hints was to convince him that he was on to something, as indeed he was. His agitation was successful; the matter was taken up by the Board of Trade and the pension scheme put on a sound footing. His superiors did not exactly victimise him, but they gave him work that kept him away from the office. For 30 years he was a travelling auditor, visiting the company's railway stations to examine the books.

John is said to have been crossed in love. That may be true, since he remained unmarried until he was 45. He never spent anything like his whole income. This was not because he was really a miser, but because he knew that, as the best paid member of the family, he was expected to help the others. His mother was not exceptional in having ten children; what was remarkable was that they all grew up. However, one of the boys was mentally handicapped, and one of the girls contracted TB. Whenever there were medical expenses, John came forward to help.

He was also prepared to help strangers. Once, on his way to work, he was stopped in the street by a man who indicated by signs that he was deaf and dumb. John bent over him, full of goodwill, to find out what he wanted. The dumb man produced from under his cape a slate, on which John read the words: 'There are some nice girls at...' The address was a good one, in the New Town.

John reeled back, and hurried to his office. There, his colleagues laughed at his horror. They said: 'Och, yon's Dummy Ingles. He's the brither o' the Lord Advocate.' John learned that the deaf mute, thinking his relations were not doing enough for him, was deliberately putting them to shame by touting for a brothel.

Shortly afterwards Dummy Ingles vanished from the streets of Edinburgh. John heard no more until he went on a walking tour—alone, because nobody could keep up with his normal pace, which was six miles an hour. One evening he came to a village so small and remote that he doubted whether he would find a lodging for the night. But a hospitable housewife made him comfortable. Over supper she said: 'Ye're no the only stranger we've seen. There's an Edinburgh man come to live here. He's the brither o' the Lord Advocate. But puir fellow! He's deaf and dumb.' John, for once, kept his mouth shut.

Because of his interest in the temperance movement, John came to know a powerful speaker and worker for total abstinence, Walter Josiah Davie. John soon realised that Davie was a hypocrite who drank in secret. But the temperance movement gave such respectability to this alcoholic that he became a professional guide, showing distinguished visitors round Edinburgh. John one day heard him boasting of his greatest triumph, the hoodwinking of the Baroness Burdett-Coutts. He had led her to Greyfriars and, on the spur of the moment, made up a tale about a dog called Bobby, who starved to death because he refused to leave his master's grave. The Baroness, Davie gleefully reported, was in tears.

No conman ever had a more lasting success. By the time the Baroness put up a statue of the dog, all Edinburgh was convinced that Greyfriars Bobby had existed. Long after Davie himself had been thrown out of the temperance movement, his creation endured. John's efforts to tell people what had really happened met with more hostility than his attacks on the kirk.

The crofters

What with his marathon walks, his official journeys and his service as a sergeant in the Volunteers (the Territorial Army of those days) John came to know almost every part of Scotland. The Gaelic he had spoken in his childhood was often useful; in the 1880s there were still Highlanders who spoke no English. But there were few Highlanders who trusted their landlords. The bewilderment of remote communities, which had allowed the Duchess of Sutherland to evict 15,000 people between 1816 and 1820, had long since vanished. Police and sheriffs were often stoned by the people they had come to evict.

On the Isle of Skye the tenants of 'The Braes'—steep, wild hillsides overlooking the sea—protested when their landlord, Lord Macdonald, took over some grazing land which they regarded as theirs. They kept back the rent. A sheriff-officer tried to serve them with summonses. The tenants forced him to burn the summonses by the roadside. Then they turned on his assistant.

The *Aberdeen Free Press* reported: 'Certain domestic utensils, fully charged, were suddenly brought upon the scene, and their contents were showered on the unlucky assistant, who immediately disappeared, followed by a howling crowd of boys.'

There were not enough policemen on Skye to arrest the tenants' leaders. With 47 Glasgow policemen (and two reporters) the local sheriff made a surprise raid at dawn on 18 April 1882. In drenching rain the police marched eight miles and got through a steep, rocky pass. Then they were surrounded.

'Men, women and children rushed forward, in all stages of attire, most of the females with their hair down and streaming loosely in the breeze', reported the *Dundee Advertiser*.

The police arrested five men, who made no resistance. It was the women who took the lead in throwing stones. The police tried to beat them off with truncheons, but for some time could not get themselves and their prisoners back through the pass.

They made it, in the end, by sprinting. '...Sheriffs and Fiscals forgetting their dignity, and taking to their heels.' The women followed, still throwing stones. The police began to throw some back.

> Scores of bloody faces could be seen...A woman, well advanced in years, was hustled in the scrimmage on the hill, and, losing her balance, rolled down a considerable distance, her example being followed by a stout policeman, the two ultimately coming into violent collision.

The sheriff got his prisoners to Portree, where the people turned out to boo the police. At the preliminary hearing the prisoners were granted bail, and returned home conducted by a piper and a Gaelic poetess. But they had to go for trial in Edinburgh.

There, they found friends. The crofters dispossessed by the Duchess of Sutherland were told by Presbyterian ministers not to resist; this was God's punishment for their sins. A very different message now reached the crofters from St. Columba's Gaelic Church, the rallying place of Highlanders in Edinburgh. One of the elders of that kirk was Norman Macleod, a bookseller specialising in Gaelic books. He was the son of a Skye crofter who died young. His mother had maintained herself and her three children by becoming the village midwife. Now he threw himself into the struggle for the imprisoned men. He could advise them because he knew the ways of the courts; he was an interpreter for Gaelic-speaking witnesses.

The crofters were not sentenced to imprisonment, but only fined. They had not, after all, resisted arrest. All the violence had come from the women, whom the papers were calling 'the Amazons'. Nobody felt like trying to arrest the Amazons. The police asked Gladstone to send a gunboat. Instead, Gladstone suggested to Lord Macdonald that he should come to terms with his tenants.

The fines, which the crofters could not possibly pay, were paid out of a fund collected by Norman Macleod. Did John contribute? Certainly the atheist and the elder of the Gaelic kirk became friends. In 1883, Norman Macleod married John's sister Flora. He had persuaded her not to go to China. Norman continued his agitation for the crofters. The next time men from Skye were in prison, he engaged a piper to stand outside and play the tunes they knew.

For him, the Crofters Act of 1886 was a fair settlement. He argued that it prevented bad landlords from doing what no good landlord would wish to do.

Fighting injustice

John, however, saw many more injustices to fight. He thought it a scandal that landlords should take vast stretches of Scotland out of use, for the sake of their grouse shooting and deer stalking. He was swimming against the tide, these being royal amusements. But he had to swim against a stronger tide in 1899, when the Boer War broke out. John had never been a pacifist; he remained in the Volunteers until he was 40. He opposed the Boer War, not because it was a war, but because it was unjust.

His eldest sister, Grace, was then living in South Africa. Her husband, Richard Adlam, was the first curator of Joubert Park, Johannesburg. Adlam supported the war, and John wrote to him explaining why he should not:

> Admitting that the Boers were conservative, narrow, intolerant and corrupt, as you say, which statements are contradicted by other authorities, and indeed by facts, how does it benefit this country to waste £100,000,000 and 60,000 casualties to rob them of their country?

That sentence exemplifies John's way of arguing. If he began: 'Admitting that…' he would then refuse to admit it. The letter continued:

> The evils of the pre-war days were surely trifles to what obtains now and is likely to obtain for many a year. You do not seem to be aware of the results of the war in the old country. Coals are almost at famine prices; works and factories are closing or working only a few days a week as the high price of coal renders work unprofitable; railway rates have had to be increased very largely, yet the shareholders of the English lines receive £500,000 less this half year in dividends. The market of the world is shifting from London to New York, where the Chancellor has to go now for part of his loan. Consols are down from £114 to £97, and the shrinking in the leading Stock Exchange securities exceeds £400,000,000.
>
> The whole of the British Army (plus 12,000 volunteers) is locked up in South Africa, and barring invalids fortunate enough to be sent home, is likely to remain there. Large drafts are leaving weekly and those troops manning the garrisons at home, Militia and Old Reservists who volunteered, are, in the opinion of the Commander in Chief, quite unfit to take the field.
>
> And the worst feature of it all is that the mob here are by interested parties excited to break up any peaceable meeting called to consider the situation.
>
> Lord Rosebery and others seem to expect that the French are going to fasten a quarrel on this country and invade us; certainly they never had such a splendid chance before to march on London.
>
> I can scarcely believe that all this is worth incurring merely that a few thousand outlanders, mostly non-Britons, should have votes in the Transvaal, and use the same to bring about on the Rand the same evils they have brought about at the Kimberley mines, where the blacks and poor whites are squeezed that the millionaires, principally Jews, should make more millions.

John would have been amazed if anyone had told him that this last sentence was anti-Semitic. In those days anti-Semitism was what happened in France and Russia. The British feeling of superiority to all other people was just natural. John always claimed to be free from racial prejudice. As will appear, his fiercest prejudices were against his fellow Scots.

How Adlam replied to this letter is not known. Probably with gratitude, because John had enclosed £25 (for present-day value, add two noughts) towards the care of Grace, who was in hospital. John was already helping another sister, Marion, a widow with three children, in her struggle to keep a small shop. (The sister with TB had died, and another sister also died unmarried.) In May 1900 the Boxer Rising broke out in China. Rebels, waving the heads of foreign missionaries, seized Tientsin. The widowed Marion cheered up and remarked: 'Och, what a peety Flora didna become a missionary! She'd have made a lovely martyr.'

Party politics and an ancestral curse

It was also in 1900 that the Labour Representation Committee was formed—the precursor of the Labour Party. John had found his spiritual home. The same year, he got married. His wife became known in the family as 'Auntie John', though her name was Georgina. They had no children, and John continued to watch over his sisters' children.

By this time girls were going to Edinburgh University. Margaret, the eldest child of Flora and Norman Macleod, did well there, joined the Socialist Society, and was remembered years later for her powerful speeches. With a good degree, she went to work for the educational pioneer Margaret Macmillan. Her brother, another Norman Macleod, was also doing well at the university in 1905, when his father suddenly died.

The hard-working bookseller left his family almost nothing. Nor could his two younger children earn anything; they were still at school. Young Norman saw that he would have to leave the university and find work. John made his usual speech about being a miser. What he offered young Norman was a business proposition. He would lend him enough money to stay on at the university, at 4% interest. Norman got his degree, took the Civil Service Examination and settled into secure, well-paid employment. He finished repaying John's loan in 1924, but his gratitude never ended. This was my father.

Grace, now a widow, returned from South Africa with her three sons, one still a schoolboy, and John settled the two elder boys in clerical work with the railway. It should by this time be clear why John's relations could never dislike him, though his views were often eccentric. For example, he distrusted anyone called Macgregor. (Or the variants: Gregorson, Gregory, Grieg and MacAra.) He maintained that the Macgregors' past, as outlaws and robbers, had given them a bias against honesty. As an auditor, he said, he always found something wrong with the books if a Macgregor had kept them.

Flora once objected: 'But don't you remember that decent man James Macgregor, the shepherd our father took with him to Mull?' 'I don't deny that he was a good shepherd,' said John. 'But he was something else. He was a dead shot. The people there still tell how, on a calm summer evening, he would take his gun to a salmon river, wait till he saw the fish jump, and then shoot it through the head. If our father had wanted any assassination done, James Macgregor would have been the man.' (Yet John himself had won awards for shooting.)

During the First World War the railway lent John to the Ministry of Food, where he exposed fraudulent claims (with particular pleasure if they came from the firm David Grieg). After the war he advocated a United States of Europe, as the way to peace. His retirement in 1920 allowed him to devote all his time to the Labour Party, and in 1924 he was adopted as parliamentary candidate for West Perthshire. This was when my father found among the archives proof of Charlie Macnab's allegation. We were descended from Campbell of Glenlyon.

John begged my father to keep quiet. If this were known, he would not get a single vote in any Highland constituency. True, Campbell of Glenlyon was well connected. Descent from him was descent from Bruce and Malcolm Canmore.

The trouble was the curse. When the survivors of the massacre ventured back into Glencoe, their hereditary bard pronounced a curse against Campbell of Glenlyon and all his descendants. The curse worked against the man; he died of wounds four years later. But his descendants were no more unlucky than other people. And surely John, the atheist, did not believe in Highland curses?

He did, though. Once he led some cousins to the top of Craigianie in Glenlyon, because this was where the MacDiarmids once dispensed justice. The footprint of St. Eonan was visible in the rock. John removed one shoe and one sock, and put his naked foot in the saint's footprint. Then he pronounced a Gaelic curse against the lady whose house was visible below. She was the Wills heiress, enriched, said John, by poisoning the workers with tobacco. The cousins stood round, giggling. A few days later the lady was rushed to hospital with appendicitis (she later recovered).

John was right about the importance of ancestry in Perthshire. When he expounded Labour policy, people traced his kinship to the MacDiarmids they knew. Wasn't his grandmother a Campbell? And his great-grandmother a Cameron? (Nobody whispered that the Cameron lady had been the great-granddaughter of Campbell of Glenlyon.) John got 5000 votes, the Tory 15,000. The Tory agent, who had estimated the Labour vote at 3000, said: 'We can't make out where the other 2,000 came from.' They had come from MacDiarmids, Campbells and Camerons.

John hoped to stand for Argyllshire, which included his birthplace, Mull. The selection committee asked for his views on the nationalisation of land without compensation. John may still have hoped to wean the workers off whisky and the nations off war, but finance he did understand. He explained what havoc this measure would cause. The committee turned him down.

He was then selected for the Western Isles. Revelling in the challenge, he said it would take him two years to get round his constituency. Some of the islands were accessible for only a few days every summer. John became popular because he campaigned for some crofters on the Isle of Lewis, sent to prison for cultivating land which they regarded, by custom, as theirs. The Hebrideans told him that he was a great candidate, but that they always voted Liberal. So, in 1929, John was defeated. At the next election the Labour Party sent a young man straight from Edinburgh University to gain practice in this hopeless constituency. To his own amazement, he was elected. Hebrideans had been thinking over John's arguments.

John's last attempt to get into Parliament was a by-election in Ross and Cromarty in 1934. He was 79. My father was furious with the Labour Party for making use of an old man in a hopeless battle. But John insisted that he was looking forward to it. He said he had seen almost every part of Scotland, but never the fine scenery of Western Ross. He did not tell my father that he had postponed a serious operation for this election.

John lost the election, but survived the operation. He died peacefully in 1937, leaving instructions for a non-religious funeral. Can an atheist have a ghost? If John McDiarmid is hovering over Scotland, he may be disappointed that the Scots are still prey to capitalists, landlords, whisky and tobacco (besides newer addictions). But as his relations meet in some exotic restaurant—even on a Sunday—his ghost should be there. It's the right place for a man who, whatever his defects, was always good company.

Extract from 'Letter to Randall Swingler'

Andy Croft

I thought I ought to drop you just a line
To let you know your life at last is done—
By which I do not mean your life but mine,
No, not *my life*, my *life of you*, the one
I've spent (my progress has been limacine
I guess) what seems like a half a life-time on,
And which is why, though you may think it daft,
I'm pleased to say you've reached your final draft.

One death's enough for anyone, I know,
And yours (which you supposed long overdue
Since the assault on Monte Camino)
Outside that pub on Shaftesbury Avenue,
The hardening artery of old Soho,
A stone's throw from the Party's old HQ,
Cannot (at fifty-eight) have been much fun—
But I can't resurrect you till you're done!

Of course, you did not ask to be exhumed,
You probably think the whole thing's quite absurd;
I don't suppose you like being disentombed,
Or waking up to find you're disinterred;
I'm sorry, also, if I have presumed
Upon our friendship, but from what I've heard
I hope you will not think me too familiar
(I'd hate to be accused of necrophilia).

I know so much about you now I feel
I know you better than I know myself;

Extract from 'Letter to Randall Swingler'

Your years of anger, war-time love's ordeal
Your wild affairs, despairs and broken health,
Your disappointed English commonweal
Remaindered like your books upon my shelf,
The only place it can be really said
We co-exist—because we're never read.

There's stuff in here I wish I'd never seen—
The failed ideals and failing hopes that start
To take on flesh beneath my spade, between
The empty bottles and the failing heart,
This lock of long-dead hair from Geraldine,
The sense of failure you made into art.
But if I'm going to dig you up the price is
Playing sexton to your many faults and vices.

I want your help, you see, I need to learn
The way you faced a lifetime of defeat
Without despair, the way you learned to turn
Dismay and doubt into a world complete,
The knack you had of knowing when to burn
Your bridges without sounding the retreat.
I need you at this century's sorry end,
And not just as my subject, as my friend.

But we've not yet been properly introduced.
Although you're dead, I feel I should explain
Just why this clumsy stranger's come to roost
Among the memorabilia in your brain.
It's dark in here, but now I'm getting used
To following the thread through your demesne,
Deciphering the desperate, antique scrawls
You left unsigned upon the blood-stained walls.

By time and place and class and education
We couldn't be more different if we'd tried,
Estranged by war and age and generation
(I was still in the Juniors when you died),
But with or without your co-operation,
Within my life of you, our worlds collide,

(I have just given you a heart-attack,
While listening to an early Velvet's track!)...

You chased the minotaur up from Salerno
To victory in 1945,
You faced it on the banks of the Volturno,
And though a part of you did not survive,
Emerging from the heat of the inferno
You showed us what it means to be alive,
And how we cannot find the labyrinth's gate
Unless we face the monsters we create.

But having killed the monster you returned
Beneath the blackened, perjured sails of peace
To find that what you hoped the world had learned
Had already been sacrificed in Greece,
To know the world you thought that you had earned
Was ransomed to appease the horned beast.
And poor Europa was again deceived
And war's next generations were conceived.

And we have lived for almost five decades
Within the shadow chill of your defeat,
Afraid to live beneath the sun, afraid
To leave our Winter's cave in case we meet
Our monster selves and know we've been betrayed
By fire-lit tales of humans who would eat
Us, lost in labyrinth dreams of cave-dark night,
Afraid to stand erect beneath the light.

I've spent too long inside this catacomb
The memories here seem mine as much as yours—
The shadows in the dormitory gloom
Familiar as the painted minotaurs
Who guard the narrow entrance to your tomb
Behind these unmarked, locked and shell-pocked doors.
And there your life and work must stay unread
Until the day the sea gives up its dead.

So this will have to do for now, old friend,

I'm sorry I've disturbed you for so long,
Although I've tried, I cannot still pretend
There's any point in trying to prolong
Your life, you're doubly dead! So let me send
You back beneath the earth where you belong,
The never-finished manuscript that says
That death's the only exit from this maze.

Note

'Letter to Randall Swingler' is included in Andy Croft's collection *Just As Blue* (Flambard, 2001).

Mapless in the Wilderness
Randall Swingler and 1956

Andy Croft

> The bomb-bud burst
> And blossomed
> And blew
> The map out of my hand.
> I returned to a strange land.
> Mapless in the wilderness.

The vivid vocabulary of comradeship and brotherhood was one of the ways in which the twentieth-century communist movement set itself apart from other political traditions. The language of friendship represented—and helped to reproduce—a genuine sense of belonging to an international movement, at the same time as it disguised the extent to which such values were routinely abused by communist parties in government. It was an easily parodied rhetorical tic and an often exploited virtue. But in a small and marginal party like the Communist Party of Great Britain (CPGB), personal friendships always had an especially significant role in helping to sustain a culture of shared loyalty. This was, after all, the organisation which Manuilsky—speaking for the Comintern—had once ridiculed as 'a society of great friends'. Party members were expected to recruit family and friends to the party; lifelong friendships, love affairs and marriages were often made inside the party. For British communists, isolated and insulated from society by the Cold War settlement, such relationships helped to compensate for the many obvious disadvantages of party membership.

For many, the crisis of 1956 was felt most intensely as a conflict between political and personal loyalties—between love of the party and opposition to the party line, between affection for individual leaders (Campbell and Pollitt in particular) and disagreement with their politics. The events of 1956 may have taken place on the grand stages of History—the streets of Warsaw, Budapest and Cairo—but their long-term consequences were played out in the lives of millions of communists round the world. Marriages and long-standing friendships were broken, patterns of hope and imagination were fractured, emotional landscapes ploughed up.[1]

The Twentieth Congress of the Soviet Communist Party (CPSU) was held in the middle of February 1956. For the new leadership it was an opportunity to launch a public reassessment of the Stalin years as Mikoyan and Khrushchev openly criticised Stalin's 'cult of personality', and the way it had deformed the administration of government in the Soviet Union. Millions of communists around the world—loyal and not-so-loyal alike—were gripped by the extraordinary spectacle of the Soviet leadership revealing ideological and personal differences in public for the first time since the show trials of the late 1930s. Then on 25 February, Khrushchev made a secret, four-hour speech in which he acknowledged the extent to which the Rule of Law had been replaced by criminal lawlessness, the Soviet Constitution by a monstrous personal despotism, and the rule of the Communist Party by the power of the security apparatus. The speech was in closed session, and the British fraternal delegates were not present (Harry Pollitt and George Matthews claimed they were being shown round a contraceptive factory at the time). But Moscow was immediately thick with rumours about the contents of the speech. Excited whisperings of incipient change began to circulate around the world, until they even reached the public bar of the Cock in the Essex village of Pebmarsh.

Pebmarsh was the home of the writer Randall Swingler and his wife, the distinguished concert pianist Geraldine Peppin. They had moved to Essex in 1951 because it was inexpensive (the Swinglers' cottage had neither gas nor electricity; water had to be pumped from a well seventy yards across the garden and carried *by yoke* to the house). But Essex also represented an escape from the compromised, half-life of post-war London, a retreat into pre-modern England, a self-imposed East Anglian internal exile.

A poet, novelist, playwright and librettist, Swingler had been the Communist Party's best-known writer since the early 1930s. He had written (with W.H. Auden) the text of Benjamin Britten's *Ballad of Heroes* and in 1939 he had filled the Albert Hall with a 'Music and the People' pageant starring Paul Robeson. Swingler edited all the literary magazines associated with the party—*Left Review*, *Poetry and the People*, *Our Time* and *Arena*, and from 1939 to 1941 he was literary editor of the *Daily Worker*. He was active in the Workers Music Association, for which he and Alan Bush wrote many songs; with Alan Bush he had edited *The Left Song Book* for the Left Book Club. He was the author of several plays for Unity Theatre, including the Mass Declamation *Spain*, the Munich-play *Crisis* and the wartime *The Sword of the Spirit*. His pageant for the *Daily Worker*'s twenty-first birthday filled the Harringay Arena in 1951. (Paul Robeson recorded a speech for the occasion.)[2]

Such visibility however, left Swingler extremely vulnerable to the discreet McCarthyite witch-hunts of Cold War London. After serving with the Eighth Army in Africa and Italy (during which campaign he was awarded the Military Medal) Swingler found himself black-listed by the BBC, witch-hunted out of university adult education, and the doors of publishers and editors closed to him. Moreover, as the Party's National Cultural Committee tried to purge itself of 'bohemian' elements, he was drawn into a series of dispiriting disagreements with King Street, disagreements which began over the direction of the party's cultural life, but which—by 1956—were increasingly expressed in political terms.[3]

Although they were always known in Pebmarsh as 'they Commyounists', the Swinglers got on well with the local farm labourers, as well as the landlady of the Cock. Moreover, they soon found themselves at the centre of a group of Fitzrovian exiles in Essex. In 1951 Swingler helped the composer Bernard Stevens and his wife Bertha move to nearby Halstead; the writer Jack Lindsay and the actress Anne Davies moved to Castle Hedingham; Geraldine's sister Mary and her husband Paddy (author of 'The Man Who Watered the Workers' Beer') moved to Pebmarsh in 1952; the following year the artist Paul Hogarth moved to the village of Little Maplestead, a mile away; two years later the composer Alan Rawsthorne and his wife Isabel (widow of Constant Lambert) moved to Little Sampford, and Jack and Amy Beeching to Twinstead. Leslie and Vivien Morton lived in nearby Clare. One regular in the Cock was heard to complain: 'It's getting that you can't order a fucking pint for all these bleeding weirdos'.[4] It was a remarkable colony of communist and radical artists, writers and musicians in flight from Cold War London. By the end of the year most of them had left the party.

The genie escapes

As early as 20 February 1956 the *Daily Worker* had been obliged to interrupt a long-running row about the politics of Burns Night in order to try to minimise the implications of the Twentieth Congress, stressing the (newly discovered) virtues of comradely self-criticism ('It's Not a Sign of Weakness to Admit Mistakes'). Over the next few weeks the paper carried a series of bewildered editorials, vainly trying to play down the attacks on Stalin. But the paper was also publishing the first letters from readers about the congress, some defending Stalin, most expressing dismay at the party's complacent response to the revelations. As if to prove the point, the editor

Johnny Campbell tried to close the correspondence after only three selections of letters. But rumours about the contents of the secret speech were now circulating Fleet Street. Staff on the paper were divided over the issue, and there were simply too many letters to be ignored. Instead of the usual pre-congress discussion (the CPGB's own congress was due to be held that Easter) the letters column over the next few weeks was devoted almost exclusively to debating the historical role of Stalin and Stalinism. Swingler joined the discussion, attacking the coverage of the Twentieth Congress in the paper and the failure of the party leadership to see the decline of the British party as a consequence of its slavish attachment to the Stalinist dictatorship, although he withdrew his letter before it was published.[5] He also wrote—with what must have been immense self-restraint—to his old adversary Emile Burns (chair of the party's National Cultural Committee):

> I wonder whether, in the light of recent developments and in particular decisions of the Soviet Party Congress, the comrades of the political committee would reconsider my suggestion of ten years ago (for which at the time I was severely rapped over the knuckles !) of issuing a book called 'The Party Line', which would analyse the method of arriving at and deciding on a line, the method of carrying it out in action, the necessity for it, and a history of the significant turns of line in the last twenty five years. When I suggested this before, you told me that such a suggestion betrayed a lack of faith in the Party and its leading comrades, because I believed that we should be absolutely honest in confessing our mistakes and showing how these mistakes came about. I thought then, and I think much more forcibly now, that the boot was on the other foot. I was quite confident that the Party could only emerge strengthened and immeasurably increased in prestige by such an open self-criticism, particularly in relation to the rank-and-file of the Labour Party. It is still true that our relations with the Labour Party are hampered by a rankling of old sores...e.g. the first phase of the War, the last phase of the Labour Government, the Yugo-slav question, the Prague Trials. Moreover—and to my mind more serious—there is perplexity and a sort of guilty conscience, even in some cases degenerating into cynicism, among a number of our own comrades in the Party which holds back the Party's growth and inhibits its work in the general political field.[6]

While most British communists were still trying to come to terms with the hideous revelations seeping out of the Soviet Union, Swingler believed they would liberate the British party from its Stalinist past and rescue a native,

English communist tradition for the future. Letters attacking Stalin and the leadership of the British party were now an almost daily feature of the *Daily Worker*. The genie was well and truly out of the bottle. On 16 March the Italian and Hungarian CPs added their voices to the denunciation of Stalin; on 17 March the Hungarian authorities announced the posthumous rehabilitation of Laszlo Rajk, and the paper ran a front- page story about Stalin's purges; two days later Campbell published a front-page summary of the Khrushchev speech; on 29 March the paper was obliged to report that *Pravda* had published an attack on the Stalin repression. Meanwhile the letters kept rolling in to King Street and the *Daily Worker* (including one from the historian Rodney Hilton, pointing out just how badly the party's cultural work had been damaged by the Soviet straightjacket). A complacent editorial on 'The Role of Stalin', insensitive contributions from Harry Pollitt, R. Palme Dutt and Willie Gallacher, and an attempt to reassure readers that political liberty was guaranteed in the British party's own programme *The British Road to Socialism* did nothing to help. Each attempt to clarify and qualify the party's relationship with the thirty-year terror in the Soviet Union left the leadership open to greater charges of complicity, deceit and double-dealing. It was clear to Swingler that the British party was not going to be able to learn from the past. He wrote an unpublished parody of King Street's disingenuous attempts at self-criticism, connecting what he called 'Emilism' to its deadly sponsor, Stalinism:

> What we need to-day is courageous re-thinking. But we must not empty out the acid-bath with the baby. We must have 'new' thinking along the 'old' lines. There are two kinds of truth, relative truth and creative truth. And we stand for creative truth, or making it up as we go along…We have made serious mistakes in the past which must now be corrected. One of the most serious was in leaving any poets, artists, musicians and such people alive at all…They are a hangover from the old world which must be eliminated. When we speak of literature, we mean Party literature, which in the form of the political statements of the Central Committee of our Party are, and indeed must be, the highest level of expression yet reached by Man, and yet in a language if not acceptable, at least accessible to the broadest and thickest masses…All these questions of Justice and Freedom which these high-minded gentlemen are continually raising in relation to the Soviet Union and the People's Democracies show how deeply they have been ensnared in conceptions of the old bourgeois order. Justice is the class-weapon of the bourgeoisie to maintain its oppressive social order. It follows that the workers when they attain power will not need any Justice…[7]

At the end of March the British Communist Party held its Twenty-fourth Congress in Battersea Town Hall. Swingler was there as a delegate from the Castle Hedingham Branch (along with the writer Jack Lindsay). Sitting in closed session, delegates heard Pollitt confirm many of their worst fears about the degeneration of the CPSU into an instrument of tyranny under Stalin, and by implication, their own collusion in mass murder. And yet the leadership and the majority of delegates were determined to demonstrate a united front to the Fleet Street vultures gathering over the congress, which ended—as always—on a note of triumphal utopianism. The old leadership was re-elected, and J.R. Campbell sent the delegates home with the confident assertion that 'an army on a victorious march does not split up easily'. 'The Communists Stand United', declared the *Daily Worker*. The crisis had apparently passed.

Leaving the party

Back in Essex Swingler reported on the congress to his branch, almost in tears, and announced his resignation. Geraldine decided to stay in the party for the time being. So did friends like the pianist James Gibb, the artist Paul Hogarth and writers like Lindsay, Edgell Rickword, Montagu Slater, Alick West and Jack Beeching. His old friend the composer Alan Bush was certainly not thinking of resigning:

> I do hope this is only a rumour. I cannot imagine you existing outside the Party, and the Party will be a sadder organisation without you, at any rate as far as many of us are concerned. Is it really true? If so, won't you let me come down and try to get you to change your mind? After all, these things are not always irrevocable. This seems to me to me the most improbable time for anyone to leave the Party. What will people here do without the Party? Muddle through, I suppose you might say. I cannot accept the idea that the British Road to Socialism will be a muddle through to it, because Socialism cannot be reached by muddle—though it may be maintained in spite of it, certainly....I still hope to live to be in at the death of capitalism in this country, and I'm sure you ditto. I can't imagine you sitting back in a rickety or even in a streamlined hire-purchase armchair. But perhaps it is all a rumour. [8]

Despite gentle pressure from old friends and comrades, it was clear that Swingler was not going to be persuaded to re-join the party. The cynicism with which Swingler now viewed the party leadership was evident when, in the middle of May, Harry Pollitt was replaced as General Secretary. His successor was Johnny Gollan, an Edinburgh Scot with a reputation for efficiency, discipline and hard work, a choice which prompted Swingler to observe that the CP was now carrying the cult of *impersonality* to extremes.

Edward and Dorothy Thompson intended to stand and fight their corner inside the party. The Swinglers and Thompsons were good friends and Geraldine was godmother to Kate Thompson, born in November 1956. Edward Thompson had regarded Swingler as the spokesman of the cultural opposition inside the party, and he now asked Swingler if he would be prepared to support a new inner-party journal which he and John Saville were planning, provisionally entitled 'Anti-Monolith'. Swingler immediately offered his support for the magazine which he thought 'a first-class idea', providing addresses for potential subscribers like the composer Bernard Stevens, James Gibb and John Berger, and offering to work as an unpaid 'distributing agent':

> I think if I were to live in a northern industrial area I would probably do the same as you, though I don't see now how London can be moved or much of the sycophantic south…The atmosphere of general turmoil seems to have slumped into a mood of sulky depression. Monty Slater shrugs and is dumb. Jack Lindsay speaks of somnambulism, 'the times seem remarkably hellish, and yet by objective standards they are probably excellent'. Jack Beeching murmurs darkly of the working class struggle being 'put back' by fifty years—on history's alarum clock presumably. Derek Kartun hisses through set teeth that he 'gives himself two months'. Paul Hogarth can't afford to think. And Alan Bush writes a remarkable letter as if nothing at all had happened since the General Strike and I had resigned from the Athenaeum because the wine was corked. As for poor Johnnie St John, he moans and wrings his hands, 'I don't know what to think or do—I must join something or I'm lost'. So I suppose he's snatched at a bunch of seaweed to cover his shame and joined up with Nausicaa Dutt's ball-playing girls again.[9]

In June the Thompsons stayed at Pebmarsh, after which Swingler went to Normandy to see John and Anne Willett. He was restless with anger and frustration, waking at four in the morning, disappearing on long walks and writing in his room. There was, he wrote to Geraldine, 'so much husk and scale of old arguments and old excuses and adaptations to be shed before I can get down to a firm realisation of what I truly think, feel and want to do, now.'[10] Swingler spent most of July in Normandy, 'getting his ideas on paper', mostly in the form of radio drama. In the hand-written notes for one of these plays, 'The Siege of Fear', Swingler compared himself to a city, besieged by guilt, self-doubt, impotence, cynicism, hysteria and despair:

> The city of Fear is besieged by Silence. They are waiting for the Spring offensive. Winter has been a relatively calm and easy time, lapped round by friendly Death. The Queen and the Archbishop counsel a devastating counter-offensive before the enemy should strike. The King is more or less paralysed with indecision and can only exert increasingly repressive measures at home. Caveat hedges between the Queen's party and the King's temporising. He counsels the greatest possible show of defensive strength, but no action. Bombax is all vindictive talk but afraid of his father, while Probus is a craven puritan who takes monkish refuge in prayers. Figura is hysterical with superstition, seeing visions and dreaming dreams...Pyx is the scapegoat Foolery, the voice of nihilist despair.[11]

He was supposed to be teaching on the London University London Holiday School in August, but there were not enough students, and so at the end of July Swingler went to stay with Nancy Cunard at Lamothe Fenelon. While he was there Edward Thompson sent him a copy of the new magazine, now called *The Reasoner*. Quoting Marx ('To leave error unrefuted is to encourage intellectual immorality') the mimeographed magazine called for a widening debate inside the Communist Party about the moral and intellectual legacy of Stalinism. The Swinglers were among the first subscribers. As the campaign against Stalin in the Soviet Union intensified, there seemed to be good reason to believe that the Cold War was coming to an end. New measures were introduced in the Soviet Union designed to guarantee political liberties, and efforts were made to switch the Soviet economy from a war footing to the production of consumer goods. Yugoslav-Soviet relations were normalised, and Khrushchev announced that there were many roads to socialism. The Berliner Ensemble visited the West for the first time with a triumphant production of *Mother Courage* in London. King Street welcomed the publication of Khrushchev's secret speech in the *Observer* and promised a special conference to 'clear the air'; articles began appearing in party publications criticising the doctrine of socialist realism; the usually-dogmatic *Marxist Quarterly* even published an essay on Gramsci; the *Daily Worker* took the Czech Communist Party to task for being insufficiently self-critical.

However, when the second issue of *The Reasoner* appeared in September—including contributions from Doris Lessing, 'Gabriel' (the *Daily Worker*'s cartoonist), Lawrence Daly and Rodney Hilton, Brecht's 'An die

Nachgeborenen' and an editorial on the need to renew the 'Case for Socialism'—the party's political committee instructed Thompson and Saville to cease publishing the magazine, since it was in breach of party rules. Comradely self-criticism had its procedural limits. Swingler poured all his outrage into a very long letter to Edward Thompson:

> What possible right can those mean-minded little squirts have to order you not to publish a socialist journal? Why don't they tell Palme Dutt to stop publishing his Labour Monthly? Theyre laughable really because they are already a long-outdated little clique representative of nobody in this country, and now dithering with fright and confusion because there's nobody to give them any instructions.[12]

But he was worried that Thompson was being manoeuvred into an unwinnable and personalised faction fight. By making the right to publish the issue on which to fight against the party leadership, Thompson was, he felt, in danger of narrowing 'the point of attack' down to a 'little factional squabble'.

That had never been Swingler's style. Unlike Thompson, he no longer believed the party was redeemable. 'I am quite convinced that there is no future in it, because it can never escape the Moscow cast of countenance and the Stalinist cast of mind'. This was why—despite Thompson's constant reproaches—he had not yet written anything for *The Reasoner*. Swingler felt that it was too much of an inner-party publication, and that Thompson had not yet recognised the impossibility of expecting anything good to come out of the Communist Party. He wanted to see the magazine turn outwards, to become a vehicle for a renewed communist tradition beyond the ruins of Stalinism. Until it became 'an open and independent socialist journal' he did not feel he could contribute to it. Swingler's thinking was still rooted within a Marxist intellectual tradition, although that tradition was now in open conflict with his long-standing adherence to the Romantic conception of the writer. The two were no longer compatible, although Swingler was still trying to stand in the place where they had once met :

> I think what is happening now in Poland and Hungary and will happen in different degrees and forms elsewhere is as much as anything the result of the betrayals of their function by socialist intellectuals. The reason why the party leaders despise intellectuals when they've got them in the party is because they know they've got the intellectuals down, licking their boots, sterilised and servile. They make a great fuss of those outside the party,

because they are afraid of them. As they should be. The intellectuals—artists, writers etc.—are the mouthpiece and the consciousness of the people. They should be the barometer by which politicians tell the political weather. They are the only means by which the outlook and feelings of that vast majority of the population who, even in a socialist state, are not primarily interested in politics and don't want political power can become articulate. At best the 'dictatorship of the proletariat' means the dictatorship of the very small percentage of politically conscious workers, who at worst can easily be coerced by the party. So that when the vast mass losses its voice, is inarticulate, and finds itself being arrogantly steamrollered by the party machine, what can it do but rise up and smash things?

Lenin was for an independent intelligentsia. In all his recorded comments on art, music, drama, etc., he made it clear that for himself he didn't really understand what was going on or what people like Kandinsky, Prokofiev, Mayakovsky were aiming at, but that the party must not interfere—or the State—in any way. It was Lenin who insisted that RAPP should be put under the supervision of the ministry of education, then in the charge of Lunacharski, who had been blasted, along with Bogdanov…in Materialism and Empirio-Criticism….Stalin was a straight philistine, whose whole aim was to wipe out the intellectuals and all originality of thought, in order to establish and maintain the military organisation of the whole country. All Lunacharski's enlightened educational system was swept away in 1930, and a sort of military curriculum with regimental discipline, compulsory study of Stalinism, frequent competitive examinations, and the whole reactionary works as even we here have managed to grow out of, substituted…Stalinism is primarily anti-intellectualism, and cannot allow any thought or intellectual expression outside the control of the Party. It's not difficult to see how this must eventually result in the exclusion of all creative thought, all human understanding, except in the sphere of the physical sciences where what is required is specific material results…

As two fundamental points of programme, I would put forward :

a) That artists, writers, musicians etc realise themselves as the consciousness of the unorganised 90 per cent, the voice of popular aspiration to which the politicians *must* listen.

b) That they never give allegiance or loyalty to anything else but the mass of the people and scientific truth.

No considerations of political expediency should ever, in a Socialist state, permit the suppression or qualification of unaccepted truth, nor

> should the State ever be allowed to feel secure. It is after all supposed to be in a condition of withering away. The answer to *Quis custodiet?* is the single-minded devotees of scientific truth.
>
> All this is such stale and banal balls really, but we have all got so much into the mentality of 'All Out Trafalgar Square Sunday' that we have forgotten what we ever started to do and why we did it...Who would ever have thought that the working masses would rise against a Communist Government in the name of freedom? We have so much rehabilitation to do in our own minds, so much rediscovery of imprisoned ideals and enthusiasms, reaffirmation of forgotten socialist and humane values...[13]

In the last week of October 1956, two popular and reforming communists came to power against the wishes of the Soviet leadership—Gomulka in Warsaw and Nagy in Budapest. Soviet troops immediately entered Hungary; when they were persuaded to leave, Nagy announced that Hungary was leaving the Warsaw Pact. On 31 October British and French forces bombarded the Suez canal; on 3 November the Soviets re-entered Hungary, Nagy was removed from office and Janos Kadar installed as leader. The response of the British Communist Party leadership and the *Daily Worker* to both events was predictable. It was not hard to find reasons to condemn Anglo-French imperialism in Egypt, but it was not necessary to find reasons to defend the Soviet invasion. All the democratic promise of the last few months disappeared in the smoke of Budapest.

The third and last issue of *The Reasoner* appeared as the terrible news came in from Hungary. Thompson and Saville were suspended, and they resigned from the party. The Stalinist reflexes of the Soviet and CPGB leaderships had survived the demise of Stalinism. Swingler was beside himself with rage and dismay. The crushing of the Hungarian 'October' was for Swingler like Cromwell's suppression of the Leveller regiments in 1649. He drafted another, unposted, letter to the *Daily Worker*:

> Socialism has gone up in the smoke from the guns of power politics. The Communist leaders in this country have abandoned at one whistle from the radio (Moscow) all pretence of socialist principle or human morality in favour of military expedience...military opportunism of a most sinister and cynical kind has taken the place of ideology or persuasion in the tactics of communist parties (hence the total reliance for internal security on secret police). Is this the 'Party of the working class'? Are these the only true representatives of the people's aspirations? 'Socialism is not for export'—no, it is now for dumping at the cannon's mouth. In the name

of honest humanity—I will not use the others you have so fouled—get you to Highgate cemetery on a pilgrimage.[14]

As the reference to Highgate suggests, Swingler was still thinking in terms of a revived communist tradition. He drafted a proposal for a new political society, modelled partly on the Fabian Society and partly on the Left Book Club, a half-way house which would take the best elements of the communist tradition into the Labour Party. It was now a necessity, he believed, for communists to make clear that the events in Budapest 'have nothing to do with Communism. The Communist idea must not go down inextricably chained to Stalinism, or Leninism for that matter'. By the end of the year over 7,000 members—a fifth of the entire membership—had left the CPGB. Geraldine left. So did most of the Swinglers' friends—Edgell Rickword, James Gibb, Bernard Stevens, the novelist John Sommerfield, the composer Christian Darnton, and James Friell (the *Daily Worker* cartoonist 'Gabriel'). Friell was something of a celebrity, and his resignation was national news; pursued by Fleet Street journalists, he went into hiding to wait for the story to die down. And what better place to hide away from the world than an ancient thatched cottage in Essex? He arrived at Pebmarsh just as Swingler was about to open a crate of whisky with the artist Michael Ayrton.

It was one way of dealing with despair. For Edward Thompson, however, Swingler was abandoning the struggle, retreating into a silence which amounted to political and moral nihilism, like the 'Nothingist' poets who after the October Revolution had written 'Write nothing! Read nothing! Say nothing! Print nothing!' Inactivity and silence, Thompson argued, represented another kind of complicity in evil. The relationship between Thompson and Swingler was, Swingler suggested, 'like one of those agonizing love-affairs where the protagonists tear each other to pieces with nightlong chains of misunderstanding until both commit suicide'.[15] Part of the problem was a generational one. Swingler felt that his young friend would not let him retreat into the silence which he felt he had earned:

> Stop it. I refuse to be the whipping boy for your thongs of sarcasm. Now clean living. We haven't got to salvage anything for them. It's for ourselves that we've got to salvage truth and compassion and ordinary human kindness, and eradicate the kind of backbiting, sneering, smearing, I'm-doing-all-the-work-and-you're-a-deserter relationship which was characteristic of C.P 'comradeship'...try to understand that I am not the embittered old nihilist you seem to think, and if I 'fail you' it is from simple incapacity and not ill-will. You have in fact all my goodwill and

admiration and always will have unless you deliberately cut it off yourself with your bitter axe.[16]

Thompson in turn accused Swingler of paranoia. He felt he was entitled to expect Swingler's support for the stand he had taken, since they shared so many of the same values and attitudes—the belief that communism was not synonymous with Stalinism, that 'historical necessity' was a 'vile imposture', that individual choices mattered, and that intellectual, artistic and spiritual struggles were not subordinate to either economics or politics. He asked Swingler to accept his responsibility for fathering so many of the arguments and so much of the 'heat' in *The Reasoner*.

Thompson and Saville were now considering what to do with all the goodwill and interest generated by the magazine. They met Derek Kartun (previously the *Daily Worker* Foreign Editor) to discuss launching a new journal, which Thompson hoped would be a natural successor to *Left Review* and *Our Time*, and which he hoped Swingler would edit. But Swingler was losing faith in his own abilities:

> I have been terribly touchy lately, since Budapest, shocked, horror-struck, paralysed. The whole thing is an emotional nightmare which I can't yet cope with—the communists torn to pieces in the streets, the steelworkers mown down in their own factories, the whole ghastly anarchy which is the harvest of unrestrained power-politics—and the pestilent wind sweeping away all our hopes and exhilarations of the summer. Because of this, and because I have had a long experience in the party of being sneered at, smeared, and generally frozen-elbowed as an unreliable element, an anti-party renegade and yes, a degenerate, I expect I have something of a persecution complex in regard to any remark or comment which seems to be 'getting at' me...Gabriel said to me when he left here a week ago, 'When you lose grip of everything else, you always find there is personal friendship to fall back on.' That is about all I have to give at present, and that not because of meanness or arrogance or *je-m'en-foutisme*, but simply because I am uncertain of everything else in myself. But I am trying to get myself straight. because I seem to contribute nothing, it doesn't mean that I believe in your 'Nothingism', but only that I don't believe in myself yet sufficiently to be able to help. [17]

Despite all this he was nevertheless prepared to help with the new magazine. He offered his services as a managing editor (responsible for layout, proofreading, circulation, advertising, correspondence, etc.) with Thompson and Saville as commissioning editors, although he disagreed with Thompson's proposal that the magazine should be published by Fore Pubs, the independent radical paperback imprint which Swingler ran with Jack Lindsay. Swingler was confident he could bring in people like Berger, Ayrton, old friends from the 1930s like Rex Warner and Day Lewis, as well as Labour MPs from the 'Victory for Socialism' group like Barnett Stross, Tom Driberg and his own brother Stephen. He suggested they 'encourage readers to initiate study groups in their home regions, which would provide the foundations of our New Socialist fellowship':

> We should publish the things that we have all been pondering, in whatever form they come, even though tentative and experimental, just as the Reasoner did, only in this case widening the range so that it is the horizon of the Socialist life which is in question, under examination, and not just the validity of a certain political party. Mainly I feel we should concentrate on the arts, their function and responsibility and the necessity of their freedom, since I hold that it is their sterilisation which has led to the total dehumanisation of politics.[18]

What Swingler could not easily give the project, however, was money. He was making a small and erratic living by abridging novels for children for the Odhams Press. 'O god! I wish I had a bit of stiff', he wrote to Thompson, 'just enough to allow freedom of movement and to get something like this going':

> Half—or more than half—my trouble Edward, and my touchiness and general inefficiency is due to the constant nagging harrying round-the-bend-driving anxiety about money, next week's money, paying the milkman, my enormous (not really but seemingly) debts—all that paralysing crap. It's an infection that kills, until you realise that it's no good fugging indoors and brooding over the dying fire of your own mind, but going out and facing the harsh west wind which blows up things like this and gets the stiffness out of your bones...Funnily enough, despair is not a state I am anywhere near now, in spite of the horror of Hungary. I have had my dose of that, in Zhdanov's time and after. I would like to try this. I would like to make amends for my bestiality. I wish I were stronger and saner. I will try to be.[19]

Swingler did, however, borrow £50 from the near-empty Fore Pubs bank account to help launch the magazine. Although Saville was unconvinced by

Thompson's enthusiasm for ex-Party writers, he was prepared to let Swingler replace him as one of the editors. 'I wd be very happy to slide out and suggest Randall in my place', he wrote, 'except that I don't think he would take my place. You do need someone who is prepared to belch and be earthy when you soar on your higher flights and you do also need someone with the physique and the psychological armour plating of a sergeant major'.[20] The Thompsons invited Swingler to their house in Halifax just before Christmas in order to meet Saville, but Swingler was working to meet the deadline on the Odhams adaptations. He spent a grim Christmas 'in a state of suspension', waiting for news of his Virgil translation, and receiving news of the deaths of several long-standing comrades and friends—Montagu Slater, Dona Torr, Ben Bradley, John Minton and Nina Hamnett. The political situation was worse than ever and 'deteriorating very rapidly, with the big Stalinist comeback' in the Soviet Union and Eastern Europe. Gabriel sent him a bottle of whisky, and Swingler wrote to thank him:

> The little world we have left seems to me to be deteriorating rapidly. The old gang appears to have abandoned all principle and aim other than sticking to their entrenched positions—where I suppose they will be left to wither away...I feel we are in for a pretty dark period in which one can do no more than keep a few clear principles alive in a small breathing space, while all these power-blockheads cut each other's throats. For all that I feel far happier and freer of guilt and frustration now than I think I've ever done, and it seems inconceivable that one put up for so long with the kind of bullying which appears to be endemic with such people and organisations.[21]

As usual, the composer John Sykes stayed at Pebmarsh that Christmas. While he was there he and Swingler wrote several songs together. 'Hope the Sower' suggests Swingler's mood that Christmas:

> Far on the rim
> Of dawn where the red arc of the sun
> Scatters the fields
> With seeds of promised light,
> Reach out the hands
> The hands of Hope the Sower.
> All wakening lands receive his power.
>
> Heavy the clouds
> Of doubt and despondency hang low

Over the world
Where men reject the sun!
Sly-lipped despair
Withers the will's endeavour.
One breath of that air destroys forever!

Oh may my heart
Respond to the promise of each dawn!
Ever my thought
Be found a fruitful soil!
That when the storm
Of doubt and fear assail me,
Deep-rooted the flow'r
Of Hope avail me![22]

Culture, politics and the *New Reasoner*

In February Swingler attended the foundation meeting of the *New Reasoner* at Doris Lessing's flat in London. Thompson, Saville, Ken Alexander, Alfred Dressler and Hyman Levy were also there. Swingler and Saville took to each other at once. It was agreed that the first issue was to carry a 'heavyweight piece' by Swingler on 'Culture and Politics' ('the creative imagination versus Stalinism'). Thompson also wanted to use a long poem by Swingler, 'The Fall of Bablyon' in the first issue; Saville was not so sure about the value of poetry, but Thompson bartered the poem for Eric Hobsbawm's 'Dr Marx and the Victorian Critics' (which he was against including). Swingler promised to ask Louis MacNeice for a poem, Claud Cockburn for 'a political effort à la Cockburn' and Bernard Stevens for an 'Open Letter to Shostakovitch'. He also suggested asking British writers to submit questions to their counterparts in Poland, printing the questions in one number and the answers in the next. He volunteered the Fore Pubs mailing lists (only to discover that they had been given to a Book Club which had rented offices from them) and offered to ask the Kenion Press—the printers of *Arena* and other Fore Pubs publications—to print the *New Reasoner*. At this point Swingler, Thompson and Lessing seem to have represented 'culture' on the editorial board against the political theorists Saville, Dressler and Alexander. Despite their disagreements, Thompson still looked to Swingler to provide the magazine with its intellectual leadership. He was, after all, the only member of the board with any experience of editing magazines, he had been in the movement longer than anyone else, and had written, published and broadcast more than the rest of the board put together. When Rickword declined Thompson's invitation to write for the magazine about Montagu Slater and *Left Review*, Swingler agreed to do it, thereby establishing a continuity between the two magazines. But by the end of March Swingler had produced neither 'Culture and Politics' nor the *Left Review* essay. Although Swingler printed the leaflets advertising a *New Reasoner* meeting at the Holborn Hall in March, he failed to turn up himself. To Thompson's immense frustration, the Swinglers did not have a telephone, and as a result Swingler could not easily be consulted over day-to-day editorial issues. Thompson decided to drop 'The Fall of Babylon' from the first issue in favour of his own 'Socialist Humanism'. He was impatient with Swingler's inability to deliver, to attend meetings or reply to letters. It was clear to Thompson that they could not rely on 'Brer Randall' for business or editorial work; the best they could hope for was his advice, the occasional poem and his wide range of personal contacts.[23]

Swingler tried to apologise for his growing 'sphynxism'. 'I'm not sure where to begin', he wrote to Thompson. 'I'm sorry for this long silence and non-co-operation, My head is like a hive of bees, all buzzing in different directions. For the last three months I have simply been thrusting irons into the fire from all sides and none are yet red-hot, or even warm.'[24] He was still busy abridging books for children, resuscitating a pre-war Group Theatre version of *Peer Gynt*, and writing a series of songs for John Sykes in homage to John Dowland. He also began work on a 'symphonic poem' for the composer Alan Rawsthorne. In April, he finally heard that the New American Library had rejected his translation of the *Aeneid*. 'Our fortunes are rock bottom', he wrote to his old friend and comrade the BBC Radio producer Reggie Smith, asking if it there was any way he could get round the blacklist at the BBC.[25] Reggie Smith pressed hard for 'The Siege of Fear' (now a parable about Cold War Europe in which a soldier, discovering that the other side are human, tries to tell his own people that there need be no war) to be produced, but it was rejected, as usual.

In April 1957 the CPGB held a special conference to 'clear the air' after the events of the previous year. Although Swingler saw it as 'the dead hand throttling the last cheep of life out of whatever true party there ever was',[26] he nevertheless followed reports of the congress in the *Daily Worker* with painful assiduity and spent that Easter drinking in the pubs near Hammersmith Town Hall while the conference took place. Jack Beeching met him on the way to the conference. 'The bus stopped for a minute or two in Chelmsford just as the pubs opened—a pint of Double Diamond at that time of day was destructive, but what Randall wanted'.[27] The conference, as Swingler expected, was a stage-managed affair, confirming the party's inability to recognise the crisis of legitimacy it now faced. The old leadership was re-elected—and another 2,000 members resigned.

After this Beeching occasionally saw Swingler at the Geneva Club, although it was hard to find him sober. The Geneva Club was a kind of proto-New Left debating society, founded by John Berger, Peter de Francia, John Willett and Swingler in 1954. Named after the Geneva Accords in the French-Vietnam War, it met in a room above Bertorelli's on Charlotte Street. Joan Rodker was secretary; members included J.D. Bernal, Margot Heinemann, J.B.S. Haldane, Barbara Niven, Miles Malleson, A.E. Coppard, Christopher Logue, Penelope Gilliat, Charlotte Haldane, Anya Bostock, James Aldridge, James Gibb, Michael Ayrton, Eric Fried, Basil Davidson, Paul Hogarth, George Fullard, Peter Peri (on whom Berger based *A Painter of Our Time*), Doris Lessing and Derek Kartun. Edward Thompson attended once; Renato Guttuso turned up when he was in London. But since Hungary—when Hugh MacDiarmid had appeared to say that he was re-joining the Communist Party—the Geneva Club had been falling apart. Several notable members of the Club like Bernal and Margot Heinemann decided to remain in the party, but most had left. Peter Fryer, who had been the *Daily Worker* correspondent in Budapest, started attending meetings after he left the party; so did Raphael Samuel. John Willett suspects that after 1956 Emile Burns tried to infiltrate party members into the Club to 'take it over'. The last time Beeching saw Swingler was at the Geneva Club:

> I was sitting between Jack Lindsay and Doris Lessing at the Geneva Club, Haldane and several other notabilities were there. A talk was to be given on Brecht, everyone was waiting for Randall who was knocking another back in the bar downstairs, and then made an entrance—convinced that both Jack and I were there on the secret orders of King Street. I had already left the party and he knew it, but by this time we were all figures in his phantasmagoria...[28]

In May 1957 the first issue of the *New Reasoner* appeared (though not on 1 May, as Swingler had wanted) edited by Saville and Thompson, with an editorial board composed of Swingler, Doris Lessing, Ken Alexander and Ronald Meek. Swingler wrote to congratulate Thompson and to exculpate himself for being so unhelpful: 'I've hardly read a newspaper—except for the strips—for weeks,' he wrote.

> I've let the side down. I haven't put in any solid Marxist thought since I last saw you, I suppose. And it's my forty-eighth birthday and nothing

done and not a bean. Not that I'm complaining for myself because the sun is warm in the orchard and we have a pair of bullfinches nesting in one of the apple trees and my wife is sweeter than all apple-flesh. But I am for you a bending, if unbroken reed…The war against the intellectuals as such is on from both sides with equal virulence. I wonder what they really did to Lukács. And what they are going to do with Dery? Humanism now means the war of little people against Great Powers. It's a losing war but can be fun while it lasts. Our orchard has become a bird sanctuary because they have cut down all the hedges for miles around and sprayed all the crops with some vile poison. There is a parable, I suppose, in this. But that doesn't excuse this incoherent excuse, and my failure to help at all. In any case it seems the start is good and may well lead, with great trees falling on all sides, to something important.[29]

'Culture and Politics' was still unwritten, and Swingler missed the July meeting of the editorial board in London. But when the second issue was published that autumn it included three poems by Nazim Hikmet translated (from the French) by Swingler, as well as his long poem, 'The Fall of Babylon'. In the poem Babylon represents imperialism and self-destructive power-politics, the fallen civilization Swingler had seen in the desolate lunar landscape of Iraq in 1942. But Babylon is also the ruined cities of the Second World War and the historical captivity in which the international communist movement found itself:

> By the waters of Babylon
> We sat down and wept
> When we remembered the mountain vision
> The agony of hope and the rigid faith kept
> Locked away in hearts too easily
> Plundered.

Babylon is a world divided by the theological differences of the Cold War, armed to the teeth for nuclear self-annihilation:

> And the Bishop had said, 'There is too much happiness.
> How shall they learn to turn to God
> Except through agony of soul?
> Come ye', said the Bishop, 'to the waters of life
> And they shall be radio-active. Suffer
> The little children to suffer

> From generation to generation.
> For the Lord of Hosts is with us
> Equipped with all the latest weapons
> Of nuclear fission.
> And He shall redeem his people
> With a single bombing mission'...

The poem ends with another form of redemption, as once again Swingler turned back to a secularised, humanist, version of the Nativity to find meaning in a world of cruelty, pride, ignorance and division:

> Ask the shaggy ass
> Or the slow cow
> Why in barest winter
> We look for a new birth
> We listen for that message
> Which light would not allow
> And the widening year disproves.
>
> Suppose we have conquered day,
> Harnessed the years of light—
> Still the protestant heart
> Drums in its own night.
> Earth speaks through the ass of the brain,
> The cow of the milky senses:
> The shepherds of imagination
> Gather their puny lambs
> Of childish understanding.
> Babylon's wise men
> Offer their several answers
> As ransom for their pride,
> But only see their own gifts.
> In the night around them
> And the naked winter
> The ass who knows he's an ass
> And the slow genitive cow
> And the unregarded shepherds
> Alone dare gaze, unflinching,
> At the tiny interrogative
> —Why?—in the dirty straw. [30]

Thompson considered the poem an example of the way the magazine could stimulate and lead the 'imaginative revival' necessary to a revived socialist politics. There was a re-alignment within the board (which now included Paul Hogarth, Malcolm MacEwen and Derek Kartun). Thompson, Lessing and Swingler wanted the magazine to carry more poetry and short stories, while the others wanted more cultural criticism. Swingler—somewhat improbably—managed to lose Doris Lessing's address and so missed the October editorial meeting. But he and Hogarth were commissioned to edit a special supplement for the third issue to mark the bi-cenentary of William Blake's birth. For once he delivered, on time. Thompson was delighted, but he disagreed strongly with Swingler's choice of 'From Islington to Marylebone' which he thought was too difficult for readers of the *New Reasoner*, and not obviously political enough. Thompson preferred the destructive, satiric aspects of Blake, Swingler the *creative* Blake; Thompson saw Blake as 'our first socialist-humanist', while Swingler insisted he was 'a lifelong repudiator of categories and systems':

> His seventy years of life span a period, like our own, when the whole pattern of human living passes through a crisis of catastrophic change : when new Energies break through old Ratios, only to form new Ratios in their turn. To Blake all systems were oppressive. He was all the time on the side of Energy…we have not behaved particularly well, in waiting two hundred years before admitting that Blake has a place among our greatest. But the Bible of Hell, or the history of the struggle of the human spirit for self-unity, we certainly have, in the total works of Blake surviving to us. And if we are only just beginning to drive a few shafts of understanding into that glowing and mysterious mine of human wisdom, it may be because we have not yet dethroned 'Urizen' in ourselves, or struck 'Los' from his chains.[31]

The Blake supplement was a triumph. But Swingler was tired of the earnestness with which the business of the magazine was conducted, weary of the whole game of politics. Failure had becoming a familiar and comfortable place. Writing to Gabriel to thank him for the usual Christmas bottle of whisky, he declared that, despite all the 'disasters, rejections, and failures' of recent years, he was 'tremendously happy, in a mad way':

> We are now so broke it doesn't mean a thing. And it's the wrong time of year. I mean there is nothing going on the land that one can pick up (ie potatoes, sugar-beet, pheasants etc). It doesn't matter very much when you

stop and consider that every hour of our day we have a hydrogen bomb passing over us—like an angel at twenty five minutes past the hour. The old place and the old people in it, are falling to pieces in a quite amiable way that provides entertainment for the local public. And every now and then, Duty (Stern Daughter of the Voice of God) sounds from Halifax to work out policy statements on culture (you know, what we do with our Elsan), for the Rising Left of Labour…I really don't know what is to become of us, and I really don't care a lot. I find there is nothing I can do. I'm unemployable. So much for a public school education. I'm not as full of spleen and anger as I was, but perhaps more full of contempt. I 'must' soon come to London to scrounge and forage—when I can borrow the fare.[32]

A few weeks later Swingler managed to borrow the train fare to meet Gabriel in London. They met John Davenport in a pub on Fleet Street, then adjourned to the Colony Club to meet MacNeice and Francis Bacon. Swingler was well known there, and Friell was made an immediate member. Friell was now working at the *Evening Standard* and 'in the money' after twenty years on the *Daily Worker*. He bought Swingler a new typewriter:

> Randall was very different from other people I met in the Party who were public school-boys, who usually had pretty safe fall-back positions—you know, they could go back to their mummy and daddy and stay a month in the country or this or that, some—extreme cases, not many—had a small income, others knew that if the worst came to the worst they could borrow a few hundred here or something like that there or go and use somebody's country cottage and so forth. Randall was really very poverty-stricken. He used to shoot pigeons and rabbits—he had a shot-gun—and pinched vegetables and what not. He trusted he would always remain a Socialist, he trusted he would always remain a Marxist, but it seemed to me he was retiring from politics. If you are a writer, what are you going to do? Go on writing in newspapers on 'Why I left the Communist Party' or 'My New Plan for Socialism' and so on? He wasn't that type of bloke.[33]

Swingler was spending a good deal of time in the York Minster, drinking with Brendan Behan. One day he introduced Behan to Paul Hogarth (as a result of which Hogarth and Behan collaborated on *Brendan Behan's Island*). Swingler was falling into a long period of careless, fruitless contentment, living a kind of peasant existence—looking after his young son Dan, pottering with unsuccessful literary projects, doing a bit of poaching, drinking in the Cock, occasionally working for local farmers or mending motorbikes, and abridging books for Odhams. The Swinglers' only real income was the money that Geraldine earned from her concerts. He would rise early each morning to cook breakfast for his son and Geraldine, then take Dan on the back of his bike to the school in the village. Not infrequently he would persuade Dan to miss school and they would go fishing on a nearby lake, or disappear for long walks in the woods behind the cottage. He was now trying to extricate himself from the *New Reasoner*. He declined the invitation to review *Dr Zhivago* in advance of its publication in English, and refused point-blank to write a paper on the 'cultural line' of the magazine, horrified by talk of developing a 'line' on anything. He was unhappy with the fourth issue of the *New Reasoner*, which debated the question, 'NATO or Neutrality?'

> Edward, the *New Reasoner* is becoming *Old Quarterly* cast in lead. Claude Roy's piece was the bright spot—apart from Dery's story—but Gosh ! The agonizing *weight* of the first half! Who's going to get through it? Or be any the wiser when they have? It's the writing—but there again the writing comes from an attitude of mind—an adjustment to life. To Life ! That's the point. You don't get any impression nowadays that anybody is concerned to do more than stop or delay, the threat of destruction to the human situation as it is—as if all wives would be satisfied, all children sane, if there were no atomic clouds over us ! We've lost our belief in life as a positive developing thing—We, the whole human race, has been hurled back by its own intellectual recoil into a defensive attitude. We're all terrified out of our wits and scrabbling in our burrows.[34]

That the magazine should be discussing a 'realistic' foreign policy at all seemed to him to be the slippery start of the 'tortuous line of slimy betrayals' which be believed they had rejected. Swingler wanted instead a 'totally unrealistic' moral policy. Anything else felt like cynical power-politics:

> Oh yes! I know what they are all going to say. What's the point of us putting forward such a policy which would never be accepted by the official Labour Party at just the time when what we want to do is to influence softly softly the said LP? What indeed? But as soon as you start out on the other tack you are caught up on the currents of 'realism' and before you know where you are you are agreeing with Bevan and tangled up in the cynical subtleties of Adenauer…crawling snail-like along the Labour Party's slimy tracks thinking we can gradually whittle this problem

down—Christ! Can you whittle down this bomber which has just passed over my head which carries more explosive power than all the bombs dropped by anybody throughout the length and breadth of the last war? Fifteen minutes, I believe, is the time allowed. Fifteen minutes for me to catch up.[35]

After more than twenty years of intense political activity and commitment, politics was now an unbearably painful absence in Swingler's life, which he could only fill with a destructive, self-lacerating guilt. He felt that he was a dead weight on the *New Reasoner*:

Edward, I am old and outdated and hating it. Last year I was briefly rejuvenated (like H.G. Wells and the Voronoff experiment) and this year comes the messenger with the notice to quit—'You are burned out and miles behind and without the capacity to catch up'—Every judgement I make is made from thirty years ago, I know that. When I read these blueprints for foreign policy I groan and take to rum. Because they are realistic—and realistic politics is now my ulcer…I can't help you—more's the pity because I am myself so corrupt with all that weak-minded phoney cowtowing to a pseudo-philosophy (which I never really accepted) for so many years…I'm sorry I'm such a weak reed. More than half the trouble, Edward, is that we are literally crippled with poverty—I mean to the point of not being able to find the fare to London and so on—and that's a vicious circle too, because in this world you get out of touch, and out of touch is out of mind and out of mind is out of job. It's my own fault. I should never have imagined this could be done, but the sort of work which comes my way has steadily diminished through the years and is now very scarce and very ill-paid. I was spoiled when I was young. It was all too easy then![36]

When Swingler again missed an editorial meeting later that year, his contribution was recorded in the minutes as the 'Silence of the Sea'. By December 1958, when representatives of the editorial board met with the editors of *Universities and Left Review* to discuss merging the two magazines, he had resigned. Swingler spent his remaining years in Pebmarsh, working as a farm-labourer, poaching, drinking too much and reviewing for the *TLS*. He died in 1967 outside the French Pub in Soho, aged 58.

While some individuals flourished outside the party after 1956, others, like Randall Swingler, slumped into despair and dismay. 1956 may have seemed for many a moment of liberation and a new political start, but for some it represented a disenfranchisement, the end of any kind of meaningful engagement in politics. For all that the British New Left emphasised the importance of cultural struggle, it conspicuously failed to generate a cultural and artistic life of its own. Although part of the New Left emerged from the 'cultural opposition' which had been gathering inside the Communist Party since the late 1940s, it was unable to survive for very long outside the party. Shaped by personalities as much as by ideologies, the post-Communist left in Britain in the late 1950s was founded on a series of tensions—between those who had joined the party before the war and a younger generation, between politics and culture, between 'realism' and utopianism, cynicism and despair. If the New Left was characterised by the close personal friendships and loyalties of the ex-Communist *diaspora*, it was also dogged from the beginning by the sapping habits of personalised rancour which they sometimes brought with them from the party. After the events of 1956, it was sometimes as hard to sustain comradeship outside the Communist Party as it was to take it seriously inside it.[37]

Notes

I wish to record my thanks to Judy Williams for permission to quote from her father's papers, and to Jack Beeching, John Berger, the late James Friell, Paul Hogarth, Arnold Rattenbury, John Saville and John Willett for helping me reconstruct this part of Swingler's life. Unfortunately Edward Thompson had to go back into hospital the day we had arranged to meet to talk about his memories of Swingler. Although I have drawn heavily on the extensive correspondence between the two men in Swingler's papers, I have respected Dorothy Thompson's request not to quote from Edward's letters. For Swingler's poetry see Andy Croft (ed.) *Selected Poems of Randall Swingler* (Nottingham, 2000).

1. For the crisis of 1956 and the British Communist Party see Willie Thompson, *The Good Old Cause. British communism 1920-91* (London, 1992), and Margot Heinemann, '1956 and the Communist Party', *Socialist Register* (1976); for events at the *Daily Worker* that year see Malcolm MacEwen, *The Greening of a Red* (London, 1991) and Alison Macleod, *The Death of Uncle Joe* (London, 1997).
2. For Swingler's pre-war career, see Andy Croft, 'The young men are moving together: the case of Randall Swingler', in John McIlroy and Kevin Morgan (eds), *Party People:Communist Lives* (London, forthcoming 2001)
3. Andy Croft, 'Writers, the Communist Party and the battle of ideas, 1945-1950', *Socialist History* no.5 (1994); Swingler's disaffection with the party was by then so public that several people assumed that Swingler had already left—'A couple of years earlier I had heard from more than one source that he was leaving, or had already left' (Alison MacLeod, letter to the author, 12 August 2000).

4. Other close neighbours included Michael Ayrton in Toppersfield, Robert Colquhoun and Robert MacBryde in Kersey, Leslie Hurry in Hundon, Bobbie and Sally Hunt in Boxford, Benjamin Britten and Peter Pears in Aldeburgh, Rene and Sheila Cutforth in Great Maplestead and Peter and Marsh Dunbar in Peb. Edgell and Johnny Rickword moved to Halstead in 1958. Two regular visitors to Pebmarsh were Hedli and Louis MacNeice, who celebrated the Swinglers' cottage in *Autumn Sequel* (1954) Canto XVI.
5. Johnny Campbell returned the letter on 30 April at Swingler's request, saying that he had been going to publish it with a reply.
6. Swingler to Emile Burns, undated letter April 1956, Swingler papers.
7. Unpublished draft, Swingler papers.
8. Alan Bush to Swingler, 5 June 1956.
9. Swingler to Edward Thompson, 15 June 1956; Swingler had already discussed with Berger and Slater the possibility of launching a new magazine which could respond to the crisis; Slater spoke at a meeting of the Geneva Club in July on 'A New Magazine Now'.
10. Swingler to Geraldine, 17 July 1956; John Willett was just back from meeting Brecht in Berlin.
11. Unpublished synopsis, Swingler papers.
12. Swingler to Edward Thompson, 26 October 1956.
13. *Ibid.* The letter from Lenin to which Swingler refers was written to Gorki on 25 February 1908; the Russian Association of Proletarian Writers (RAPP) was the dominant organisation in Soviet literary life between 1928 and 1932; Swingler appears to be referring to Lunacharsky's defeat of the sectarian 'Proletcult' groupings in 1924.
14. Unpublished letter, Swingler papers.
15. Swingler to Edward Thompson, 22 November 1956.
16. *Ibid.* Cf. the correspondence with Thompson quoted in Doris Lessing, *Walking in the Shade. Volume two of my autobiography, 1949–1962* (London, 1997).
17. Swingler to Edward Thompson, undated letter November 1956; for Thompson's relationship with Swingler see Andy Croft, 'Walthamstow, Little Gidding and Middlesbrough: Edward Thompson, adult education and literature', *Socialist History* no.8 (1995); see also E.P. Thompson, 'Outside the whale' in *The Poverty of Theory and Other Essays* (London, 1978), 'Christopher Caudwell' and 'Left Review' in *Persons and Polemics* (London, 1994).
18. *Ibid.*
19. *Ibid.*
20. John Saville to Edward Thompson, 29 November 1956.
21. Swingler to James Friell, 29 January 1957.
22. Unpublished poem, Swingler papers.
23. A number of people closely associated with Swingler were later published in *The New Reasoner*, notably Paul Hogarth, Jack Lindsay, Bernard Stevens, Arnold Rattenbury, James Boswell, Gordon Cruickshank, John St John, Bobby Hunt, Tom McGrath and John Berger.

24. Swingler to Edward Thompson, 27 May 1957.
25. Swingler to Reggie Smith, 11 April 1957.
26. Swingler to Edward Thompson, 25 January 1957.
27. Jack Beeching, letter to the author, 4 March 1993.
28. *Ibid.*
29. Swingler to Edward Thompson, 27 May 1957
30. *New Reasoner*, Autumn 1957
31. *New Reasoner*, Winter 1957/8 ; the Blake supplement also included Thompson's study of 'London' (as 'Marion Jessup'), which many years later he expanded in *Witness Against the Beast* (1993).
32. Swingler to James Friell, 22 January 1958
33. Interview with James Friell, 8 November 1993; according to Jack Beeching, Swingler was never at home in the post-communist New Left; 'he could see the awfulness of many of the disillusioned/newly-illusioned…his new world was not the one he wanted it to be, and what did that leave but the booze? In a gloomy sense it may have been his class position and the privileges that formerly went with them that at the last dislocated and betrayed him' (letter to the author, 27 December 1999).
34. Swingler to Edward Thompson, 9 May 1958; he also wrote an unpublished essay for the magazine, 'Atomphobia', along these lines.
35. Although Swingler often spoke for a part of Thompson's own instinctive responses (he even offered to publish an essay based on this letter, 'What About People?' in the *New Reasoner*), Thompson felt he also had to mediate between the 'realists' and the 'utopians' on the editorial board; the essay was never published.
36. Swingler to Edward Thompson, 9 May 1958.
37. For the birth of the New Left see Michael Kenny, *The First New Left. British intellectuals after Stalin* (London, 1995), Bryan Palmer, *E.P. Thompson: Objections and Oppositions* (London, 1994) and Fred Inglis, *Raymond Williams* (London, 1995).

John Saville and the *Dictionary of Labour Biography*

Interview by Malcolm Chase

Malcolm Chase's interview with John Saville marks the publication of volume 10 of the *Dictionary of Labour Biography* and John's retirement from the editorial chair.[1] The interview took place at the University of Leeds on 3 July 2000.

MC Seeing the ten volumes, there is a huge range of material from Joseph Mather (born in 1737) through to Alan Merson, communist intellectual, dying in 1995. I didn't add up the number of entries, but there must be close on a thousand. How does it feel, relinquishing direct responsibility for it?

JS Well, I don't feel bereft in any way. The *Dictionary* has always been, as it were, part of my intellectual life but it has never been really the most important part, curiously enough, and I worked almost exclusively in the evenings on the *Dictionary*. Naturally I thought it very importan to get the whole thing straight and right and so on. I have regarded the *Dictionary* as an important part of my intellectual life; but I assumed that I would get to ten volumes and I assumed I would stop. I think it important for historians of the labour movement—a good deal more useful than I anticipated when I first began. But in terms of my own work, it is of equal importance. It is not the major thing that I have done in my academic life or political life.

MC Looking back at how the *Dictionary* has developed, are there things you would have done differently in retrospect?

JS No, I don't think so. I don't think volume 1 is very good, volume 1 includes Ramsay MacDonald but that was because the author was a great friend of mine and a good liberal;[2] but I think after volume 1, I got a feel of the structure that we needed and I think the straight answer to your question, which must sound a bit overbearing and arrogant, is no. I think from volume 2, the structure basically has not changed except for the substitution of the special notes for specialist bibliographies. Remember when I started, labour history was not taught in universities. I think in 1960 there probably was not one course in the whole country inside universities, there might have been in adult education but I don't think there was a single course in 1960. By 1970, things were beginning to change and specialist bibliographies were coming about. I think the special notes are an extraordinarily important and welcome addition because they do deal with events and issues which otherwise, I think, in a lot of cases would simply get omitted. I refer to the Labour Party delegations to Hungary, etc. which I think were very important indeed and do tend to get forgotten, and things like the 1917 Club—people refer to it but nobody knew anything about it. So no, let me come back again to your question, I think from volume 2, the structure remained the same. Of the innovations that I introduced into biographical dictionaries, I think probably the subject index may well be the most important single one.

MC It is certainly the element that reviewers refer to, as allowing an extraordinary degree of flexibility and widening the possible readership of the *Dictionary* to people who may have no interest in the labour movement whatsoever. I guess that the advent of machine readable text, on CD-ROM, will change that but it does seem to me that in a pre-computer era, the subject indexes at the back have immeasurably increased the usefulness.

JS Two points about that. One is that nobody ever talked to me about subject indexes. I talked to a lot of people and nobody ever mentioned this. It came to me about six months before we were due to send the completed script into Macmillans. The thing that has always remained with me is the question, 'So how many coal miners were Primitive Methodists?', and it was that question that led me to say, well of course you have to have a subject index in every volume. It seems now so obvious. It was not so obvious in 1970.

MC Your view is that volume 1 has imperfections but with volume 2 you had got it as you want it. Nonetheless, I notice leafing through the editorial forewords that in volume 3, you do say that the size of the volume is reduced, the costs are rising and that the editors could no longer 'be held to previous undertakings'. What, if anything, was lost of the earliest vision?

JS I have no idea.

MC Not a lot by the sound of it!

JS I don't know, I mean I have absolutely no idea. I think that it may well have been Macmillans talking about the cost, but I am not at all certain and I cannot remember this. It is a complete blank and I do not believe actually that volume 4 or 5 were all that different from previous volumes. Did you think that?

MC Well, the number of entries comes down, but then the size of the entries goes up.

JS That's right. One of the important differences it seems to me between the *DLB* and the *Dictionary of National Biography* is that the *DNB* always gives you a word limit and I never did that. There were some entries that I sent back because they were too long but, by and large, I have been increasingly prepared over the years not to mind how many words there were, as long as it was a decent entry. I wrote an entry on Maurice Dobb and it came to 7,000 words! The fact is that Macmillans never argued the question of length. Your comment about volume 3 worries me mildly, but I don't remember any serious conflict at all with Macmillans, they have always taken what I have given them and been very helpful.

MC Why did Macmillan publish? Were they your first choice?

JS No, I had an agent, Rubinstein, a well-known agent. It was suggested to me that it would be quite sensible to get an agent and I did and they were very helpful. He must have got Macmillans but as far as I know it was never offered to anybody else. I have had very amicable relationships with Macmillans: they have simply taken what I have sent them. I can't remember any arguments. You are quite right about the numbers getting fewer because of the length of entries, but that was my decision. I did cut some down from the editorial side but mostly not. But, as I say, I wrote 7,000 words on Dobb and what I did, I let other people do.

MC One of the other striking things looking across the *DLB* as a whole is how the coverage of women is increased, less than two per cent of the entries in the first volume, more than sixteen per cent in the latest. Was there a conscious decision on your part to seek out people who might contribute entries on suitable women subjects?

JS Yes, to some extent. Somehow or other I never had any problem filling a volume, people either got in touch with me or I got in touch with them. I was after all very much involved in labour history circles. I was a founder member of the Society for the Study of Labour History, which still goes on, and I was chairman for some time. I knew pretty well most people in the UK. I also developed quite close relations with a number of people in the United States and Canada. Canada was important for me. And also, and most importantly, so was the International Institute for Social History in Amsterdam. I was given quite a bit of help in general but by and large I never had a problem of wondering, 'could I fill this volume?'

MC So the increase in coverage of women perhaps reflects greater activity among historians and awareness of women's contribution?

JS Absolutely. Obviously, I must have been affected, as we all have been, by the development of feminism in general and feminist history: obviously, we have all been part of this changing climate of opinion, so it could come from both sides. I think the real answer to your question is that I was simply part of a lively academic community in the 1960s and 1970s, and I had no problem in finding people who wanted to offer entries, whether they were men or women.

MC Is there anything missing from the first ten volumes that you feel should be there?

JS I don't think I have ever thought in those sort of terms. There are a whole range of people whom I would like to see, but from quite early days I had assumed that the *Dictionary* would go on and on, and that ultimately most of the important people would get covered. That's one aspect of it. The other is that we started collecting material on anybody and everybody and there are a very large number of files that are three-quarters completed in terms of collection of material about the individual. So that I don't think I had to scratch around thinking 'X ought to be in', because I said to myself, 'X will be in in due course, and X may well be among the many files for whom we have started collecting material'.

MC One omission I suppose has been the Trotskyite strand within the British labour movement.

JS Now that's very interesting, yes. I felt that too. Do you know I have never, ever, been offered any entry by any living Trotskyist about Trotskyism? Isn't that interesting? I know quite a lot of Trotskyists and I know most of the Trostkyists who are concerned with labour history. I have always been amused that no Trotskyist has ever offered one of their own kind to be written about, and there are a number of people I would be very happy to include. But I was just amused at this—I knew that they would go in ultimately. So let me say emphatically: a) I have never been offered anything and b) if I had been, I should have been happy to accept it. There may well have been arguments about style—that's another matter; but in principle there would be no question that I would have accepted it. It's interesting, Malcolm, that you have picked that up because that has always been in my mind.

MC I have to confess that it is the only gap I can really find.

JS Who would you include?

MC Well, I suppose Jock Haston.

JS Well, of course Jock Haston. I got all his material after he had left Trotskyism and he went very right-wing. He gave me his papers and 3,000-odd pamphlets now in the university archives at Hull.

MC So there obviously is a corpus of material in the whole archive for people to work on?

JS We may well have, I can't say yeay or nay, but we may well have, I am sure we have a file on Haston and those files will now have gone to the new editors. But there are other Trotskyists I can think of who would deserve an entry.

MC Could we look a bit at the origins of the project? Looking at other European countries there is nothing comparable to the *DLB*, except perhaps the *Dictionnaire Biographique du Mouvement Ouvrier Français*, which predated the *DLB*.[3] Was that the direct source of inspiration?

JS No, it wasn't. I got to know Maitron, the editor, through François Bédarida who was, I suppose, the outstanding French scholar of English history after Halévy in the modern period. I got quite close to Maitron and in fact Joyce Bellamy and I did a two-volume biographical dictionary which was translated into French by Maitron's institute.[4] I don't suppose you have ever heard of it.

MC I was vaguely aware that there was a French dictionary. I don't suppose there are many copies in the UK.

JS No, I don't imagine there are, but it did include living people, because Maitron's own dictionary included living people.

MC So the primary inspiration then for the project was the files you inherited from G.D.H. Cole?

JS No, I don't think so. The primary stimulus undoubtedly came from within the Communist Party Historians' Group. When I came back from the Army in 1946, I was in London because I had a job with the Civil Service while looking for an academic job; and I worked for a man called James Jeffreys who was doing a little book for Lawrence and Wishart in a documentary series. He was doing 1850 to 1880 and Eric Hobsbawm did the later one. That was the beginning of my entry into the CP Historians' Group and it was the ten years from 1947 to 1956 of the CP Historians' Group which greatly enlarged my own intellectual horizons and sharpened my wits, my historical wits anyhow. In general I thought this the most productive, useful and helpful period of my intellectual career. There was a Classical Group, a Medieval Group, and a Seventeenth Century Group around Christopher Hill (which was the most important I think). There was no Eighteenth Century Group until George Rudé came in and he didn't come in very much, and then there was a Nineteenth Century Group, of which really I think only Eric Hobsbawm and myself were academics. There were quite a number of teachers.

What we got out of this was of course the recognition that history from below, the story of the struggles of the ordinary people, unorganised and particularly those organised, had been grossly neglected and it was our job to remedy this. So I had ten years of this. I had written *Ernest Jones*, I had edited a volume for Dona Torr on 'democracy and the labour movement', I had edited with Asa Briggs the first *Essays in Labour History* (which is the best volume I think), which was of course for Cole's seventieth birthday; but he died and so it was a memorial.[5] So I was, as it were, steeped in labour history in general. When Margaret Cole offered us these files, I said 'Yes, I will see what I can do'. (Asa Briggs was going off to Sussex and he said no.) So without really having anything in my mind, certainly nothing of a large-scale objective, I said yes, and it really took me most of the 1960s to work the thing through. I mean I started in ignorance and I gradually, I hope, dispelled that ignorance as I worked through. I have, in fact, written in the introduction to volume 10, 'Un peu d'histoire', of some of the problems I encountered. It wasn't really until the end of the 1960s, that I really got the feel for the structure that I wanted. But I was doing a lot of other things too and I repeat what I said at the beginning: while I always thought the *Dictionary* very important indeed, politically and historically, and I enjoyed it, it never dominated my life.

MC Can you say a little more about, as it were, the 'inner circle' of collaborators and contributors to the *Dictionary*, beginning obviously with Joyce Bellamy who was there, presumably, some years in advance of volume 1 being published?

JS Oh yes, about three or four. I do write about her [in the introduction to volume 10] and I hope I have given a generous tribute to Joyce. She was not an historian, but she had a quite extraordinary commitment to any job she was given. Everything she did was meticulous and she was also one of the best copy editors you could ever want. She was extraordinary, but I never had any intellectual discussions with her about it because she was not an intellectual. She was not an historian, she couldn't really tell whether an entry was very good, good or not acceptable, but that wasn't her job. I mean she was just wonderful, she worked five-and-a-half days a week, six if necessary, and was a most extraordinary person to have as a research assistant; and one final thing, she obviously didn't agree with me on a number of issues but she never argued. She might make a gentle comment but she would never get uptight. And there were times when I regret I grossly neglected her because I was doing other things and she went on steadily: there was always work to be done. She was a quite remarkable research assistant and the *Dictionary* would not have appeared had it not been for her, as I explained in my introduction, 'Un peu d'histoire'. But it was my responsibility in the last resort. I did the argument with authors, I decided whether we would take an entry or not—we did refuse some—but we tried to be reasonable. I had a lot of argument with lots of people about this and that and about interpretation. There were about three or four that, in the end, I actually turned down. Now that over 35 years is not bad.

MC Somebody else, obviously more peripheral than Joyce, but whose name catches the eye as one looks through the earlier volumes is Anthony Elliott.

JS He was wonderful.

MC Did his work on political biography beyond the labour movement find an outlet anywhere?

JS No. He died from a heart attack, he was appointed ambassador to Israel and was swimming somewhere, the Red Sea I think, and he had a heart attack and died. He was a marvellous man, he was one of these kind of diplomatic guys, full of good manners, very bright, lively. Why he started collecting biographical material on all MPs was that when he was at Eton when he was 18 or something, he read a Left Book Club volume called *Tory M.P.* by Simon Haxey (which was a pseudonym). Elliott told me that it was reading that that got him going. He was extraordinary, and I think I quote in my obituary that when he got to Israel, he said 'I have discovered in Tel Aviv a complete run of the *Jewish Chronicle* or whatever for the nineteenth century or twentieth century and I shall be able to look up all kinds of people'. He was obviously very busy as an ambassador but he always wrote fairly soon after I wrote to him. I thought he was absolutely wonderful and I miss him very much.[6]

MC Somebody else who obviously was a major source of help and informed criticism in the early volumes is Margaret Cole.

JS Oh yes. I saw a lot of Margaret Cole. I can remember one occasion when I took her, I think to the Arts Club, somewhere just behind Charing Cross Road, and we had lunch, and she said, 'See me back to my car': she was tight. I was very worried about her. But you had to be very careful with Margaret Cole. If you didn't reply to a letter within 24 hours she would expect an explanation. She was a tough old woman, but she and I got on well. She could be very rough and I have seen her being very rough with people, but she and I—and I watched my step very carefully—were very close in the sense that we liked each other. You had to watch your step very carefully always with Margaret, but she was helpful, and she was pleased with the *Dictionary*.

MC One of the other names that pops up in the editorial forewords, and you speak of him very warmly after his death, is Philip Larkin. You actually said in volume 8 that he had been a consistent support for your work and had arranged special grants for purchase of material for the library. I guess some people reading that would be surprised, in that Larkin's is not a name that one would automatically associate with a particular warmth and interest in labour history.

JS Oh no, he was very right-wing—he talked about my 'subversive archive'. What happened was that about 1960, or a bit earlier, I discovered that Cole had a very close relationship with the International Institute for Social History in Amsterdam. I discovered to my surprise that Douglas Cole was in fact encouraging people to deposit their papers in Amsterdam and they had got quite a lot of interesting stuff. And in particular I learned that Raymond Postgate, who was of course his brother-in-law, had given his General Strike leaflets and pamphlets and so on, and I thought well for God's sake, if we're trying to build up labour history in this country, this is not the thing to do. We need to collect our own. Who's doing it? I talked around, for example, in the Society for the Study of Labour History. So I decided that that was one of my jobs. This has no real connection with the *Dictionary* but in terms of time it was parallel. I don't know what the first acquisition was, but then I got the Jock Haston material. I got an introduction to Haston, I am almost certain, through Stuart Hall who I was involved with in the New Left. Anyhow the Haston papers were the beginning of the labour archive. Now the interesting thing was that Larkin saw the point of building groups of archival material. We had almost none and I started collecting and so by the middle 1960s there was quite a lot and Philip then realised they should be catalogued.

Then of course I had this wonderful discovery about 1968 of the Union of Democratic Control [UDC]. To cut the story short, I worked at the UDC when I was unemployed (I got a First in 1937, didn't get a research scholarship at the LSE as I expected and was out of work). Dorothy Woodman (I forget how I got in touch with her, she was living with Kingsley Martin of the *New Statesman*) was secretary of the UDC and I used to go there and work part-time. She paid my fare and gave me a bit for lunch but that was all. I did it very happily. Anyhow, in 1968, the committee of the UDC, Jim Mortimer was in the chair, decided to close the organisation down because it was out of date and they advertised that a university or some other institution could have their papers. I learned about this but didn't do anything that summer because I was busy. Then the UDC wrote to two specialists who would give them advice. Of course their committee couldn't make up their mind: the papers had been applied for from Nuffield, from Sussex, and from one other, I have forgotten who the other was. The two experts they wrote to were Edward Thompson and me, and they said 'who would you advise?'. Edward Thompson wrote back and said, although LSE hadn't applied (and they didn't and there was nobody at LSE interested), the UDC papers ought to go to LSE because they've got E.D. Morel's papers, and E.D. Morel was the first secretary. I wrote back a thoroughly academically immoral piece; I said 'Thank you for your letter. I would like to suggest that neither, or none of your three candidates should be given them, but that they should come to Hull because Hull is the place that is actively collecting and we have got a librarian who is interested'. I'd already got the papers of the National Council for Civil Liberties. Larkin had to buy this subversive archive and he did—he was always supportive of our labour archive.

But coming back to the UDC. I wrote my letter and that was all. Two or three months later, our assistant deputy librarian, a man called Wood, got a phone call saying 'would you come and collect your papers from the UDC?'. He didn't know anything about it. So he said 'OK, how big is the file?'. 'It's three quarters of a shelf'. So Wood told Larkin and Larkin told me. I said to Larkin: 'This is absurd. I know the UDC and I know their files, they go back to 1914 and they're terribly important. They've got Russell, they've got MacDonald, they've got a lot of interesting people in their correspondence'. I said to Philip, 'when I heard this my nose twitched'. So Philip said 'Well, OK, go to London and you can get rid of your twitch', those were the words he used. I went to London to a great house in South Kensington (in what had been an upper middle-class area) and went in to the ground floor where the new secretary, he had only been there three years, was present. Now the UDC had made two moves, one from Victoria Street where I worked, and then to Southampton Row and five years earlier to this place. The Secretary had not been there when they moved because he only came three years later, and he was the only one there. Two corners of the big room was UDC, the third was the Socialist Medical Association, and the fourth was the Eugenics Society, or at least I thought it was. So, we looked around for an hour and a half, nothing. We looked in every cupboard. Clearly he was getting sceptical with the fact that I had come down from Hull. So I looked around and I went to the Eugenics corner and there was a big filing cabinet, but behind it was a great mahogany door. So I said to this bloke, 'What's that door? What's behind there?'. He said 'I don't know, it's never been open since I've been here'. I said, could we look? He said yes, but he was very reluctant. Anyhow we moved the cabinet. We opened the door and it was a dark cavern and we hadn't got any torches. When we lit matches there were five feet of documents!

MC An extraordinary story.

JS Yes, wonderful. And Philip said fine. The interesting thing about Philip was that in his working day his politics did not intrude. Moreover, he actually had the best atmosphere in the library that we have ever had. If people were ill, he would visit them. I have been very healthy but when I had a hernia Philip came to the house to see me. You see none of this comes out at all in Motion's biography of Larkin.[7] He misses entirely the fact that he was a very good librarian and everybody was terribly happy with him—not just the women he slept with. There was a better atmosphere at the library than there has ever been since. He was very good, and you know with my 'subversive archive', as he referred to it, he was very happy to help in any way he could. So we've got a very good labour archive at Hull.

MC Summing up then, the *Dictionary* has obviously involved a huge commitment to the organisation of other people's intellectual effort. Ralph Miliband, in the tribute to you in *Democracy and the Labour Movement*, said that he suspected that that this was at a cost to much original research you might have done of your own.[8] When we were talking earlier, you were quite categorical that you saw this as an important part, but not the most important part, of your academic career. Are there things you had to postpone or not do at all because of the amount of time that the *Dictionary* took up?

JS Well, I could have done much more of my own, I mean on Chartism. The book I published on Chartism and the state in 1987 I could have published in the late 1960s.[9] But I also had a family of four and I had no money. My salary was good but we had no capital and I did a lot of extra work. For example I did a lot of work for Augustus Kelly of New York. He published reprints: it was my doing that shifted him from publishing economics classics to publishing a lot of labour history as well and I was paid. I did a number of introductions, quite long ones, to reprints, most of which are on the library shelves but nobody mentions them. So no, I don't think so. The last fifteen years in any case I drifted away from labour to international history. My last book was the *Politics of Continuity* which was the study of the Labour government 1945–51, the damnation of Ernest Bevin.[10] And on that I wish I had more time. I wish I had started earlier. I would like to go on living for another ten years and then I might be able to produce another two more books on foreign policy. I think that looking back the outstanding feature of Britain since the Second World War has been the subjection of Britain to American foreign policy.

MC I think that is the perfect point at which to end, but are there any aspects of the *Dictionary* that you think ought to be brought out in this interview that we have not covered?

JS I think that the most important thing is that it was the Communist Party Historians' Group that really stirred me intellectually. I mean I had got a First, I wasn't an idiot, but meeting people like, you know, Hill, Hilton, Hobsbawm, Dona Torr and lots of others, made those ten years very exciting intellectually and I think they were very important for me. Secondly people are very nice, people are very helpful, my relations with my contributors have been very happy. It tells you a lot about the human nature of academics. They are a mixed lot I know, but I have been fortunate in my various colleagues who worked or offered things for the *Dictionary*. Very few were unpleasant (there were one or two, but I can take that). Mostly people have been very happy and very willing to discuss and that kind of thing. They behaved as scholars should behave. So it has been a very happy part of my life and, I think, very important. I have enjoyed it.

Notes

1. John Saville and Joyce M. Bellamy (eds), *Dictionary of Labour Biography*, vol.10 (Basingstoke, 2000).
2. C.L. Mowat.
3. Jean Maitron, *Dictionnaire biographique du mouvement ouvrier français* (Paris, 1964–1993).
4. Joyce Bellamy, David Martin and John Saville, *Dictionnaire biographique du mouvement ouvrier international. Grande Bretagne* (Paris, 1979).
5. John Saville, *Ernest Jones, Chartist. Selections from the writings and speeches of Ernest Jones with introduction and notes* (London, 1952); *Democracy and the Labour Movement. Essays in honour of Dona Torr* (London, 1954); *Essays in Labour History*, vol.1 (Basingstoke, 1960).
6. See also John Saville, 'In memoriam Anthony Elliott, 1921–76', *Dictionary of Labour Biography*, vol. 5 (Basingstoke, 1979), p.ix.
7. Andrew Motion, *Philip Larkin. A writer's life* (London, 1993).
8. Ralph Miliband, 'John Saville: a presentation', in David E. Martin and David Rubinstein (eds), *Ideology and the Labour Movement. Essays presented to John Saville* (London, 1979), pp.15–31.
9. John Saville, 1848: *The British State and the Chartist Movement* (Cambridge, 1987).
10. John Saville, *The Politics of Continuity. British foreign policy and the Labour movement, 1945–46* (London, 1993).

Reviews

Books to be remembered (2)

British Soldier in India: The letters of Clive Branson, London, 1944

This is a somewhat unusual volume in the English literature on India. These letters were not written for publication but were the domestic correspondence between Clive and his wife, Noreen. They were collected together and published after his death, at the age of 36, when he was killed fighting the Japanese on the Burma front in late February 1944.

Clive Branson had been born in India, his father being an officer in the Indian Army. Clive was two years old when the family returned to England where he entered upon a typical upper middle-class lifestyle. At the age of 18 he persuaded his parents to allow him to enter the Slade School of Art in London, and for the next few years he was wholly absorbed by his artistic work. In April 1931 he met Noreen, a young woman who at the time was a music student, and within two months (on 1 June) they married. By this time Clive had begun to find his way into the politics of the left, and after brief periods in the Labour Party and then in the ILP he joined the Communist Party. When the Spanish Civil War began in the summer of 1936 the Bransons, like all the political left, were deeply involved in the various Aid for Spain movements and in the spring of 1937 Clive volunteered to join the International Brigade. Early in 1938 he arrived in Spain and a few months later his company was captured by a section of the many Italian troops of Mussolini fighting for Franco. Life in prison was hard but in November 1938 he was among an exchange of British prisoners with Italians.

He was called up into the British Army in January 1941 and because of his politics, which he never concealed, he remained in the ranks. He lectured, whenever he could, on his experiences in the International Brigade. In March 1942 he found himself on a troopship for India—a long journey in those days round South Africa—and again he lectured some eight times on the International Brigade with a specially prepared one for a group of officers.

Clive Branson found India exciting, full of colour which as an artist he appreciated more than most, and in the poverty and physical degradation of so many of its people, deeply disturbing. In March 1943 he was posted to the gunnery wing of his unit in the town of Ahmednagar (which happened to be his birthplace) and he soon had made contact with an Indian art master and his family. He became very close friends with Kelkar, the art teacher, and he drew and painted members of the household and their friends. When he was posted back to his unit he left with much regret from everyone. His letters on this period are especially interesting.

Clive was a close observer of the Indian scene and its society but there were two themes that were especially important and he writes on both in vigorous and sympathetic language. The first was a matter of principle which closely engaged him and it is clear from the way he writes and describes what is happening that he felt it important to underline the morality involved. Racist attitudes were common among the soldiers of the British Army in India. No one in India during the war could fail to be aware of the unpleasant attitudes towards the 'wogs', mostly outside the bazaars and cantonments which were under some degree of control by the Army itself. Clive always stood his ground inside his own unit and in general, and it was not always easy. But what troubled him most was the poverty and misery of so many of India's millions. He happened to be travelling through Bengal when he left his friends in Ahmednagar and this was in the late autumn of 1943 when one of the worst famines of the twentieth century was being inflicted upon the people of Bengal. The extract which follows illustrates the vigour of his writing and the nature of the terrible tragedy being suffered :

> The last part of my journey was like a nightmare. The endless view of plains, crops, and small stations, turned almost suddenly into one long trail of starving people. Men, women, children, looked up into the passing carriages for their last hope for food. These people were not just hungry—this was *famine*. When we stopped, children swarmed round the carriage windows, repeating, hopelessly, 'Bukshish sahib' with the monotony of a damaged gramophone. Others sat on the ground, just waiting. I saw women—almost fleshless skeletons, their clothes grey with dust from wandering with expressionless faces, not *walking*, but foot steadying foot, as though not knowing where they went. As we pulled towards Calcutta, for *miles*, little children naked, with inflated bellies stuck on stick-like legs, held up empty tins towards us. They were children still—they

laughed and waved as we went by. Behind them one could see the brilliant fiendish green of the new crop.

These letters of Clive Branson are the vivid expression of the anti-imperialist minority of the British people. They are a necessary part of the history of Britain that one day will receive its scrupulous recognition. The letters were sent to a young woman who throughout her life continued her commitment to the politics of the left. She has worked for many decades for *Labour Research*, the indispensable monthly for industrial relations in all its many aspects, and in her later years she also found time for serious research into the history of the Communist Party from 1927 to 1951, published in two volumes. Early last year Noreen celebrated her ninetieth birthday.

Clive and Noreen Branson: names to be honoured and remembered.

John Saville
John Saville is professor emeritus at the University of Hull and president of the Oral History Society

Note

There is an entry for Clive Branson in J. Saville (ed.), *Dictionary of Labour Biography*, vol. 2 (Basingstoke, 1974), pp.53–62.

Living politics

Mary Davis, *Sylvia Pankhurst: A life in radical politics* (Pluto, London, 1999), xv+157pp., ISBN 0-745-31518-6, £10.99 pbk.

Mary Davis' new account of Sylvia Pankhurst is a brave attempt to chart the life of one of the more complex figures from British women's history. Pankhurst had many involvements during a life which began in the radical culture of Northern England in the late nineteenth century and ended with a state funeral in Ethiopia in 1960. Davis has dealt with this by selecting one aspect of Pankhurst's life, her political activism, as the focus for her book.

This focus certainly makes Pankhurst a more containable subject, and Davis' study has much to recommend it when placed alongside other attempts at reconstructing her life. It is more adventurous in its scope than Barbara Winslow's Pankhurst biography which effectively finishes in 1924, whilst its single-authored format lends it much more coherence than the useful collection of essays edited by Ian Bullock and Richard Pankhurst which cover the same chronological period.[1] Davis' decision to focus on the political aspects of Pankhurst's life also saves her work from some of the more strained explanations of her sometimes contradictory behaviour which appeared in Patricia Romero's picture of Pankhurst.[2] This is largely useful, although there are occasions within the text where some conjecture would have been helpful in exploring Pankhurst's motivation for her political decisions.

The first chapters of the book deal with Pankhurst's involvement in the suffrage movement, first through the Women's Social and Political Union (WSPU) and through her breakaway East London Federation of Suffragettes (ELFS). Here, Davis has taken little account of much recent suffrage historiography in constructing this picture, preferring to take her analysis uncritically from the view of the WSPU presented by Jill Liddington and Jill Norris.[3] Consequently, Davis reiterates much of what she finds bad about the WSPU, presenting it as undemocratic, anti-socialist and overtly middle-class in its composition, which raises the difficult (and here unanswered) question of exactly why Sylvia remained in this organisation until her expulsion. Recent revisions of the WSPU have demonstrated it to be a complex, fluid body, especially at branch level, and Davis' Pankhurst would sit surprisingly comfortably within it.

The later chapters on Pankhurst's Communism and anti-fascism are more convincing although more personal analysis would have been welcome, especially when attempting to explain the factionalism which led to Pankhurst's expulsion from the CPGB. Davis questions why her subject clung so firmly to her own line, but ultimately fails to present an answer. The anti-fascist material invites easier handling as Pankhurst's vocal criticism of imperialism before 1914 allows Davis to present some continuity of motivation here, and her work for Ethiopia following Mussolini's invasion is usefully contextualised.

Overall, Davis provides a useful introduction to Pankhurst. Readers unfamiliar with Pankhurst will learn much that is less well-known about her, especially concerning her work beyond the suffrage campaigns. The omission of much recent suffrage historiography does detract from the book's usefulness as a teaching text, but it nevertheless offers a concise and readable account of Pankhurst's political work.

Krista Cowman
Krista Cowman teaches history in the School of Cultural Studies at Leeds Metropolitan University

1. Barbara Winslow, *Sylvia Pankhurst. Sexual politics and political activism* (London, 1996); Ian Bullock and Richard Pankhurst (eds), *Sylvia Pankhurst: From Artist to Anti-Fascist* (Basingstoke, 1992).
2. Patricia W. Romero, *E. Sylvia Pankhurst. Portrait of a radical* (London, 1987).
3. Jill Liddington and Jill Norris, *One Hand Tied Behind Us. The rise of the women's suffrage movement* (2nd edition, London, 1999).

Sartre and the effects of war

J.-P. Sartre, *War Diaries: Notebooks from a phoney war 1939–1940*, transl. Quentin Hoare (Verso, London, 1999), 366pp., ISBN 1-85984-238-0, £15.00 pbk.

'The war', Sartre told an interviewer in 1975, 'really divided my life in two.' How right he was. Before the Second World War, Sartre's commitment to personal freedom and his determination to realise his mission as a writer resulted in a rejection of any political commitment. And yet, a few years later he emerged as the epitome of the politically committed intellectual. The clue to this radical transformation of self lies in his war-time experiences.

In September 1939 Sartre received his call-up papers and was dispatched to Nancy, in eastern France. For the next eight months, when France was officially at war but there was no fighting, Sartre was part of a meteorological corps attached to an artillery HQ in Sector 108, just behind the front in Alsace. Shunted about from small town to small town to the east or north of Strasbourg, Sartre's duties were far from onerous (to say the least) which meant that rather than killing Germans he was faced with the prospect of killing time. And this he did in the way he knew best—by reading, thinking and writing. His writing, which came to over a million words, included letters penned *daily* to his mother, to Wanda Kosakiewicz—his current inamorata—and Simone de Beauvoir, as well as other correspondents, and working on what was to become *The Age of Reason*. In addition, he kept a series of notebooks.

Between September 1939 and March 1940, Sartre wrote, in all, fourteen notebooks which were designed for future publication—albeit posthumously—and it is five of these which comprise the collection published in this volume. Although an incomplete record of this singular period, (at war but not at war), these five notebooks nonetheless offer a fascinating account of his daily life, of his reactions to the books he was reading, and of his thoughts, ideas, and reflections. These notebooks, here in a brilliant translation by Quentin Hoare, also provide a unique insight into the initial stage of Sartre's transition from an apolitical writer to a politically committed one.

Before the war, Sartre was, in his own words, 'installed in my situation as an individualist, petit-bourgeois writer'. Until 1939, Sartre had believed himself to be sovereign, enjoying 'pure freedom', but it was through the negation of his own individual freedom occasioned by his conscription that he became aware 'of the weight of the world', and of his links with all those other conscripts and of their links with him. Thus began Sartre's discovery that he was 'a social being.'

During the Phoney War, Sartre came to the realisation that it was no longer credible to 'abstract' himself from history. During his sojourn in Germany from 1933-1934, for example, he had written nothing about the rise of Nazism. On his return to France he had refused to vote for the Popular Front or become involved in any of the anti-fascist committees, or any of the support groups for the Republican cause in Spain. It was only as a conscript during the Phoney War, as he later told de Beauvoir, that he 'began to reflect upon what it meant to be historical, to be part of a piece of history that was continually being decided by collective occurrences…That made me become aware of what history meant to each of us…Each one of us was history.'

Thus, during the Phoney War, Sartre came to realise that political events were not simply a backdrop against which he could play out his individual desires and aspirations. He was a part of history and history was part of him. This revelation was linked to his discovery, through his reading of Heidegger, of authenticity. Whereas, before the War, Sartre had believed that being authentic was being 'true to oneself', irrespective of the socio-politico-economic context within which one found oneself, now he realised that the situation in which one finds oneself is all-important. In Notebook Three (11 November–7 December 1940) he wrote: 'To be authentic is to realise fully one's being in situation, whatever that situation may be.' (p.54)

Sartre's reflections and readings led him to conclude that he could no longer stand apart from politics, could no longer ignore the political context in which he found himself, but that he had to embrace his situation and become an actor within it. This meant he had to reject the pre-war ' free-floating, free individual'; he had to go beyond his pre-war self, and reinvent himself in the light of his new discoveries. Referring to his pre-war self, he described himself as 'an abstract, rootless individual…"up in the air" with no ties, having known neither union with the land through work in the fields, nor union with a class through solidarity of interests. 'I feel', he wrote, 'no solidarity with anything, not even with myself: I don't need anybody or anything. Such is the character I have made for myself, in the course of thirty-four years of my life. Truly what the nazis call 'the abstract man of the plutodemocracies. I have no liking for this character, and I want to change. What I have realised is that freedom is not the Stoic detachment from loves and goods and all. On the contrary, it supposes a deep-rootedness in the world.' (Notebook 14, March 1940, p.293)

Sartre took the lessons he learned during the Phoney War, the realisation that he was a social being, his discovery of authenticity and historicity which linked freedom and responsibility, with him though the rest of the war—

and beyond. It informed the play *Bariona* written and performed in his POW camp in December 1940, after his capture in June. It inspired his creation of the resistance group *Socialisme et Liberté (Socialism and Freedom)*, formed shortly after his release from captivity in March 1941, and his resistance play *Les Mouches* (The Flies) which was staged in Paris in 1943. Indeed it underpinned his post-war passionate advocacy of political commitment.

Sartre's *War Diaries* offer therefore, besides an account of his day-to-day life as a conscript, an indispensable insight into the process of politicisation of France's greatest intellectual. The only regret is that Verso were not able to include Notebook 1 (September-October 1939) which surfaced in 1991, and was published in French in 1995.

David Drake
David Drake teaches French at the University of Middlesex

Ordinary people, different lives

Jeffrey Weeks and Kevin Porter (eds), *Between the Acts: Lives of homosexual men 1885–1967* (Rivers Oram Press, 1998), ISBN 1-85489-093-X, xiii+190pp., £9.95 pbk.

Between the Acts is a collection of fifteen life stories, based upon interviews with homosexual men born between the 1880s and 1920s. Conducted in 1979 as a research project exploring the development of homosexual identities and subcultures, these interviews were first edited for publication in 1991. They are, as the editors emphasise 'an exceptional resource...insights into a crucial period when the documentary sources are limited'. In comprehending homosexual lives between 1885 to 1967—when all male homosexual conduct was illegal—Weeks and Porter move away from *cause celebre* and literary memoir, offering 'interviews with ordinary people from a variety of class, occupational and geographical backgrounds'.

On one level these are simply another addition to the historical record, opening marginalised sexual practices and cultures to scrutiny. All permit analysis of the ways in which same-sex desire was understood and identities structured through interaction with wider social formations. They afford a glimpse into the negotiation of legal and social prescription. It becomes possible to discuss the development and organisation of queer social networks in metropolitan London, in relation to patterns of urban sociability and economic and cultural change. John for example points to the role of monetary exchange, Roy to 1930s meeting places. All this considerably enriches our understanding of the sexual, social and cultural landscape of late nineteenth and twentieth century Britain.

Between the Acts has further interest as a work of community history. It locates contemporary sexual communities within a continuity of same-sex desire, giving that community—and the struggles for queer rights—a sense of past. Weeks and Porter acknowledge this, offering 'this book to our readers in the belief that the[se] lives…provide a bridge between a past that is fast fading and a future still to be made'. As historical practice gives legitimacy to the present, so present pride gives weight to distant voices. The text is dedicated to the interviewees 'who have had to wait so long for their memories and experiences to be validated'. If these men invoked Wilde or ancient Greece to establish an authentic cultural presence, so contemporary queer communities invoke *their* experiences.

These are organised into a narrative of collective struggle, honouring 'those who lived in difficult times, morally and culturally but survived, sometimes with great pain but often with enormous pleasure and growing pride'. *Between the Acts* represents the process by which 'people gained confidence to speak out, to reveal what was generally covert…to share common experiences'. Yet the opposition between past isolation and present community constitutes a peculiarly Whiggish history. This belies the experiences gathered here. Sam does not describe marginalisation and isolation but revels in a world in which queer men were a central and recognisable presence. History is more complex—more in need of exploration—than Weeks and Porter allow.

There are more fundamental problems, arising from the assumptions on which the interviews rest. First is the commonality of experience assumed to derive from the legal situation. Theoretical prescription conflicted with operational and cultural constraints upon police practice and the ability of queer men to step outside official surveillance. Law enforcement focused upon specific sites (cottages) and behaviour (the effeminate 'pansy'). For those able to access domestic space or members only clubs the risk of arrest was much attenuated. The experience of illegality was fractured by class, age and knowledge. If arrests were a persistent feature, particularly of working class lives, other oral and written material suggests many men lived through the period oblivious to the legal situation.

This assumption is part of a generalised process that subsumes the differences between queer historical subjects. In part Weeks and Porter recognise this, noting that 'the interviews do not…reflect the whole range of male homosexual experience'. Yet there is more than mere sample bias. Most of the interviewees were contacted through gay political organisations. All conceived of themselves in 1979 as homosexual and of their sexual desire as an innate and dominant factor in structuring their own identity. Their stories are organised around a narrative of significant transformation, the moment at which their homosexuality was identified and realised.

Such historical practices—as Scott Bravmann suggests—'reify certain current cultural conceptions of homosexuality' which 'elide the multiple differences among gay men'. *Between the Acts* projects contemporary assumptions about sexual difference and identity into the past. The period between 1885 and 1967 is thus 'eighty-two years when homosexuals…inhabited a…twilight world'. In this schema same-sex desire was historically organised and understood around the binary opposition of homo- and heterosexuality. Yet George Chauncey's work suggests that such a sexual regime is a strikingly recent phenomena. Chauncey points to the organisation of working class sexual behaviour and identity around categories defined by gender roles—not sexual object choice—and to a regime in which male-male sexual encounters contributed to a man's gender status.

Understandings of same-sex desire outside the homo-hetero binarism are thus marginalised in this representation of the past. Certain points of tension in each narrative reveal this. Gerald comments on the 1920s 'at that time there was no talk about homosexuality…I…didn't realise the significance of it'. The lack of homosexual self-conception is read as absence—not as the presence of alternative sexual understandings. Sexual behaviour outside contemporary definitions of homosexuality—dockers having sex with men whilst maintaining steady relationships with women—can only be explained in negative terms. Norman perceived the Guardsmen with whom he had sex as *not* homosexual and purely venal in motive. He—and *Between the Acts*—failed to recognise the multiplicity of queer experiences and identities, fractured according to race, class, gender and politics.

There is no simple resolution to this problem. Married 'heterosexual' men who participated in homosexual encounters in their youth do not come forward for interview. Changes in the organisation of sexual behaviour mean this important and exciting volume should be handled with care. Sexual difference must be understood for the ways it was historically produced and experienced. Past categories of sexual difference are not those that organise our lives today.

Matt Houlbrook
Matt Houlbrook teaches English at the University of Essex

A childhood coloured red

Judy Kaplan and Linn Shapiro (eds), *Red Diapers: Growing up in the communist left* (Chicago, University of Illinois Press, 1998), 320pp., ISBN 0-252-02161-4, £47.50 hbk; ISBN 0-252-06725-8, £18.95 pbk; **Phil Cohen** (ed.), *Children of the Revolution: Communist childhood in Cold War Britain* (London, Lawrence & Wishart, 1997), 224pp., ISBN 0-85315-841-X, £12.99 pbk.

The opening of the Soviet archives in the years following the collapse of the USSR has encouraged renewed scrutiny of the 'high politics' of the international communist movement and its constituent national parties, in both eastern and western Europe. Historians, both sympathetic and hostile, have looked to discover in the voluminous files of the CPSU incontrovertible evidence that might settle the central controversies that have long animated communist party historiography. Much of this work has been concerned with the intricacies of 'the line', and the mechanisms of ideological and organisational control that were employed to enforce it from the Kremlin downward.

Yet these newly accessible records now being pored over by eager researchers provide, on their own, a partial and inadequate account of the experience of communist party membership. The resurgence of these traditional institutional accounts has been challenged by the rise of a parallel historical method that draws on the traditions of social, cultural and oral history to flesh out alternative accounts of party life.

The two examples of this latter genre reviewed here introduce the perspectives of children who grew up inside communist and leftist families in Britain and the United States. In *Children of the Revolution*, Cohen presents, in a series of thirteen interviews, the oral testimony of thirteen 'Cold War babies' whose childhoods were shaped, to varying degrees, by the political commitment of one or both parents to the work of the Communist Party of Great Britain (CPGB). Each prefaced by a brief biographical sketch, these reflections on the experience of communist childhood are 'meant to be a cross-section who give a flavour of what a CP upbringing was like, in as much as one can use that generic description.' (p.11) *Red Diapers* offers the written autobiographical accounts of forty-six 'communist children' who either grew up inside, or whose families were 'involved in political, cultural or educational activities led or supported by' (p.2) the Communist Party of the United States of America (CPUSA).

Despite the obvious differences that distinguish the political and social environments in which British and American communist families lived and struggled, both before and during the years of the Cold War, these accounts touch on unusual aspects of 'growing up red' that appear to have been common on both sides of the Atlantic. Many contributions describe the thrill of feeling special and different from school friends and neighbours, and the excitement that came from a sense of belonging to something secretive and misunderstood by others. This notion of otherness could produce, as its unwelcome corollary, feelings of resentment about the obstacles that it placed in the way of fitting in. The culture of the party, with its rallies, marches and social events could reinforce that feeling of community and separateness; yet these obligatory rituals could also be tiresome, and onerous. Most contributors make reference, to varying degrees, to parental absence (both physical and emotional), and discuss the impact that their father's and mothers intense political commitment could have on the conduct of 'normal' family life. Several describe the chaotic freedom of a disordered home life, something that could be the result either of intermittent parental attention or conscious parental choice. Others regret the degree to which the disciplines of 'democratic centralism' intruded into family relationships. Some reveal their pride that they now feel for their parents' determination and personal acts of sacrifice. Others reflect on the multiple costs—both to their parents and to themselves—of their revolutionary ambitions. A few speak openly of their sense of emotional neglect, and of the miseries of a childhood endured in the low self-esteem encouraged by their parents decision to prioritise the cause ahead of their immediate familial obligations. The shock of parental disillusionment with the party, and the often agonizing soul-searching that preceded a decision to leave its ranks, is explored by a number of contributors who recall their efforts to understand their parents' sense of loss or of relief. The complications that communist teenagers faced in rebelling against parents who themselves claimed a dissident identity is discussed in a number of different stories of adolescence, both by those who, in adulthood, have absorbed the politics of their parents, and those who have rejected them.

The intention of Cohen's work on the children of CPGB families is to present an illuminating selection of life-histories that document different elements of a 'communist childhood'. Because Cohen makes no greater claims for his study beyond the contention that these experiences are worth recounting, its value can only be judged on the selection of interviewees and the strength of the testimony that they provide. Cohen certainly presents an interesting mix of party children, including Brian Pollitt, son of the CPGB leader Harry Pollitt; Nina Temple, the party's last general secretary; comedian Alexei Sayle; and children's author Michael Rosen. But although Cohen is clear that his selection should not be seen as representative, it would have been useful for him to account in some way for his choices, and the process that led him to them. The highly readable testimonies themselves contain moments of real interest and insight. They might, however, have been strengthened had Cohen chosen not only to edit, but also to develop, the narratives from his original interview transcripts. At times these can appear fragmented and even repetitious. While it could be argued that these texts provide a more authentic account than the polished literary biographies offered in *Red Diapers*, it does seem a shame that so many intriguing themes are introduced, but not pursued, here. In a brief introduction Gillian Slovo, reflecting on the familial consequences of her own parents' commitments to communist politics, highlights important concerns that are sometimes mislaid in the life-stories that follow. Cohen's own commentary can't claim to isolate what it is that might have distinguished a communist childhood from one defined by parental commitment to any other all-embracing political, social or religious ideology, but his reflections on the paradoxes of the experience are apposite.

Red Diapers is a more ambitious, and on the whole a more successful, piece of work. In their introduction the editors address questions concerning the credibility of the accounts they are presenting, discuss the fallibility of memory, and acknowledge that these life stories can only communicate an account of 'the truth' that is 'partially remembered and partially constructed'. (p.7) The book is organised into three thematic sections, within which the stories are presented chronologically. 'Family Albums' addresses the diverse home lives and the web of family relationships within which 'red' babies from across America were nurtured and raised. 'Political Trauma as Personal History' reflects upon the impact that anti-communism and political persecution had on the lives of children whose parents were its targets, and its victims. There is an emotional intensity to this section—replete with stories of desperate children haunted by the fear that their parents would soon meet the same fate as the Rosenbergs—that nothing in Cohen's book could be expected to match. The third section, 'Claiming Our Heritage', explores the different ways in which 'red diaper babies' have, as adults, reassessed their childhood years and reflected on the political maelstrom in which they grew up. The range of reactions is as wide as might be expected. Some condemn their parents' political commitments in harsh and accusatory recollections defined by feelings of rejection and exclusion. Others celebrate with relish their memories of 'growing up red', taking inspiration from the life of their family and its political community, and revelling in the identity of an outsider. Most tread a middle path between these two reactions, striving to reclaim and reinterpret what they see as the positive elements of their unusual past, yet willing to set aside other less palatable ones.

Kaplan and Shapiro's book is a more rewarding and engaging read, not just because of the quality and the diversity of the accounts that it presents, nor simply because the dilemmas facing families of the CPUSA in the dark paranoia of the McCarthy years make for more dramatic and disturbing testimony than that provided by the more mundane travails of the CPGB. Taken as a whole the stories in *Red Diapers* highlight many of the cultural, social and political conjunctions that together shaped the complex experience of 'growing up red'. Yet this is the cumulative effect of reading dozens of separate life-stories. The editors of both these works forego the opportunity to distill any general conclusions from the pages of testimony that they have compiled, choosing instead to let these autobiographical voices speak for themselves. Such an approach can, of course, be viewed positively, for its refusal to cram a complex and rich tapestry of life-stories into a simplistic sociological or behavioural model. Negatively, it might be seen as frustratingly incomplete. Communist party historiography will certainly be all the poorer if those promoting an alternative to traditional institutional accounts feel an automatic obligation to set aside any claim to analyse or comment on, the testimonies that they gather.

Richard Cross

Richard Cross is completing a PhD on the CPGB 1977–1991 at the University of Manchester

Between social reformism and Soviet communism

Bob Reinalda (ed.), *The International Transportworkers Federation 1914–1945* (Stichting beheer IISG, Amsterdam, 1997), 301pp., ISBN 9-068-61124-0.

From its earliest inception European labour movements understood their struggle for the emancipation of the working classes as an international struggle transcending (in theory) not only national borders but also confines of ethnicity, race, religion and gender. Yet everywhere these same labour movements developed within national contexts which had a profound nationalising impact on these movements' leadership and rank and file. Internationalism hence (in practice) often appeared as a kind of afterthought to the 'real' struggles of Labour carried out almost exclusively within national contexts. However, in this marvellous centenary history of the International Transportworkers Federation (ITF), the editor Bob Reinalda and his fellow contributors remind us that there were genuine internationalists and internationalism in the European labour movement who deserve to be remembered, all the more so, as they often belonged to a social revolutionary tradition of European socialism which was as far removed from the social reformism of Social Democracy as it was from the pseudo-revolutionary rhetoric of Soviet Communism.

A total of 26 chapters (some of which are only a few pages long) organised in five sections provide excellent insights into the political, organisational and ideological world of the ITF. The editor himself sets the scene by providing, in the first section of the book, an overview of 100 years of ITF history, paying special attention to both its current agendas and organisation as well as to its early history before the First World War. When European nationalism and imperialism culminated in the madness of war in 1914 it also broke the neck of Labour's internationalism. However, the ITF, like most of Labour's various internationals, was reconstituted in 1919 at a meeting in Amsterdam. The charismatic Dutchman Edo Fimmen (1882-1942) was appointed general secretary, an office he held continuously until his premature death in the midst of the Second World War. During this period, his undogmatic left-wing socialism decisively shaped the outlook and policies of the ITF. Hence the second section of the book is devoted almost exclusively to Fimmen (see especially the biographical sketch of Fimmen's life written by Sigrid Koch-Baumgarten) and some of his key co-workers in the ITF (those who get special attention in the book include Nathan Nathans, Max Zwalf, Jacobus Oldenbroek and Omer Becu).

The ITF's position within the international labour movement is discussed in the third section of the book. The tensions between national and international commitments as well as conflicts surrounding differing professional and political interests in the international seamen's organisations of the ITF are the topic of Hartmut Rübner's article, whilst Reiner Torstorff investigates the complex relationship between the ITF and the Communist trade union International. Geert van Goethen looks in detail at the debates surrounding the question of international working-class organisation, in particular the question whether trade secretariats such as the ITF (formed by national trade unions) were superior to a combination of national confederations such as the IFTU. Reinalda considers the ITF's and especially Fimmen's anti-imperialism and his concern for bringing the workers of the colonial world into the organisational orbit of the ITF. And the editor also examines the success of the seven individual sections of the ITF in achieving practical improvements for transport workers in the inter-war period.

The ITF, however, never was narrowly concerned with typical trade union issues which is why section four of the book is devoted to some of the major political campaigns of the ITF. It was, after all, one of the prominent frontline organisations in the battle of the Left against fascism. There are chapters on the economic boycott against the Horthy regime in Hungary in 1920 (Máté Molnár), on the attempt to prevent the shipping of weapons to Poland in the same year, when Poland waged war on the Soviet Union (Reinalda), on the fight against Italian fascism (Stefano Maggi), and on the extensive struggle against German and Spanish fascisms (Dieter Nelles). Nelles' article deserves special praise. In a meticulously researched article, he draws on his wide-ranging knowledge of the ITF's resistance against European fascisms to provide a densely argued overview of its many and diverse underground activities.

In the final section of the book the war-time activities of the ITF receive further attention, especially its co-operation with war-time American intelligence and its planning for the reconstitution of European trade unionism in the post-war period.

Overall, this book provides a fitting tribute to the socialist internationalism of men such as Edo Fimmen. All contributors combine high standards of scholarship with a clear and accessible prose style. Thus the unfolding of the exciting story of the ideals, values and practical politics of an international trades federation in the first half of the twentieth century becomes a powerful reminder of a socialist tradition which could serve as a basis for the renewal of a socialism that deserves its name in contemporary Britain and Europe.

Stefan Berger
Stefan Berger teaches history at the University of Glamorgan

A Soviet introduction

Richard Sakwa, *The Rise and Fall of the Soviet Union 1917–1991* (Routledge, London, 1999) ISBN 0-415-12290-2), xviii+520pp., £17.50; **Stephen J. Lee**, *Stalin and the Soviet Union* (Routledge, London, 1999), ISBN 0-415-18573-4, ix+130pp., £6.99.

One of the historian's most important skills is the ability to gather, assess and order raw information to develop and support a case. History students in further and higher education are constantly exhorted to make use of primary sources in their assignments, and their eventual grades often depend on the extent to which they do so. British students, however, are notoriously inept at foreign languages. This can be a serious problem where most of the primary sources are not in English. These two books from Routledge provide students of Russian history with translations of original documents. They are not intended to be read from cover to cover as integral works of history.

Richard Sakwa's book is the more substantial of the two, and is aimed at university students. It consists of documents and excerpts from documents grouped into chronological periods, introduced and linked by short explanatory passages by Sakwa. It starts with examples of pre-1917 revolutionary literature, to give some insight into the ideological background to the Soviet story. It continues the narrative through 1917 and beyond, ending with Mikhail Gorbachev's valedictory speech at the end of 1991. The documents presented include official party and government statements, speeches, factional literature, and dissident and oppositional material. There is also a good bibliography and a useful index.

The biggest problem for Sakwa must have been in deciding which items to include and which to leave out. No two historians of the USSR will ever concur on this question. Certain areas are definitely under-represented. In particular, there is very little material relating to the non-Russian parts and peoples of the Soviet Union. The experiences of Moscow's non-Russian subjects from 1917 are a vital factor in explaining the fall and disintegration of the Soviet Union.

Sakwa's introductory and linking passages provide the necessary context to allow students to use the documents. However, these passages are rather sparse in places. Here and there terms unfamiliar to most students, such as "Populism" and "Legal Marxism", are used without explanation. A little more detail, or an expanded glossary, would have been very helpful to the intended readership. There are also a few irritating minor errors (such as the dates of Trotsky's birth and the construction of the Berlin Wall) which should have been ironed out. Overall, though, this book presents a varied and well-translated collection of material which deserves to be widely used by students of modern Russian and Soviet history.

The focus of Stephen J. Lee's *Stalin and the Soviet Union* is much narrower. Lee's book is aimed at A-level students, and its structure is very different. It is divided into subject headings, rather than chronologically. The excerpts from primary sources are much shorter, and serve mainly as illustrative material for longer "analyses" which set out the historiographical issues in the form of mini-essays. These could be useful for students who wished to cheat on their homework, so long as their teacher was unfamiliar with the book. These analyses present the historical debates well enough, but they also contain a number of inaccuracies and questionable assertions. Of course, this might help lend plausibility to any cheat's denial of plagiarism. For example, Lee refers to Georgians in World War II initially welcoming the German armies as liberators (some might well have done, if only the Nazis had got as far as Georgia). He writes that Leningrad was "recaptured" (it was never taken). He also states that Stalin "helped put Hitler into power". That can certainly be argued, but it really needs to be demonstrated rather than baldly asserted.

Stalin and the Soviet Union contains some worthwhile material for further education students, if used as a study aid along with other works. It also has a good index and helpful bibliography. However, given the obsession with exam results in British further education, it is most likely to be used to cram A-level candidates with stock answers intended to satisfy their examiners.

Francis King

Francis King is a part-time history tutor at the University of East Anglia and a freelance translator

Far more than pool and ping-pong

Bernard Davies, *From Voluntarism to Welfare State: A history of the youth service in England, volume 1, 1939–1979* (Youth Work Press/National Youth Agency, Leicester, 1999), xii+212pp., ISBN 0-86155-208-3, £14.99 pbk; *From Thatcherism to New Labour: A history of the youth service in England, volume 2, 1979–1999* (Youth Work Press/National Youth Agency, Leicester, 1999), xii+207 pp., ISBN 0-86155-207-5, £14.99 pbk.

Early on in his work, Davies states that one of his ambitions is to describe the history of the profession to which he has dedicated his life *in context*. His history involves an attempt to locate changing practices and policies 'in the (changing) ideas and social, economic and political conditions of their time, and in their broader educational and social policy contexts. Youth work, youth organisations and the youth service itself are thus treated, not as special or exceptional but, first and foremost, as examples of the way educational and welfare activity has been organised and *institutionalised* in our society'.

Would be readers should be clear that this work organises a great many detailed analyses of policy debates and organisational developments, which will be mainly of interest to those with connections to youth work. Its achievement is to work outwards from these, and illustrate the links between issues 'internal' to the field and the wider context, rather than to tell the story of sixty years of society using youth policy and youth work as an illustrative vehicle.

These two volumes cover a wider range of activity than the general reader might assume is covered by the term 'youth service'. Whilst most volunteers, part time workers and full time staff *have* been involved in running youth clubs at evenings and weekends, there's been much more to the work than providing pool and ping pong for bored teenagers.

Davies' valued contribution as a writer, teacher, worker, union activist and consultant in this field has always involved drawing attention to its ideological and political dimensions, and such careful considerations shape this history. He traces the story of how forms of youth work rooted in philanthropy, charity and evangelism came to be shaped by government concerns about the condition of youth and their prospects during and after the second world war. The central role of the local state in providing or supporting youth clubs and other projects in the context of a broadly educational context dates from this period.

A large part of Davies' first volume is given over to consideration of the Albemarle report and its context. This 1960 government document formed the basis for the professionalisation and expansion of youth work during the sixties. This parallelled the wider growth of education and the emergence of the teenager as an increasingly autonomous and powerful consumer, and subject of moral panics. Sensitivity to youth culture, an awareness of social trends and issues such as 'the generation gap', and a concern to encourage young people in their personal and social development, were all signalled in Albemarle, partly as a consequence of the role of Richard Hoggart in drafting the report, along with Leslie Paul, who'd founded the Woodcraft Folk, the youth organisation linked to the Co-operative Movement.

The political moods and developments of the 1960s and 1970s further shaped the nature and role of youth work and the youth service. Influenced by radical and counter-cultural movements, as well as by the liberal and tolerant values shaping many social policy developments during these decades, many practitioners increasingly saw the importance of working against forms of oppression, and of advocating for young peoples' rights and encouraging and facilitating the 'empowerment' of youth.

The gathering momentum of new right politics through the 1970s provided a context within which such values were never going to be allowed their full expression, and the profession began to struggle to achieve high levels of self-confidence, a clear sense of direction, and unambiguous political support. Davies traces the debates around various government policies and initiatives, and the changing cultures around training and in the infrastructural organisations of the profession. He finds that there were a lot of important issues being debated—and he has his own views on those issues. But he reflects that 'the either-or debates' which rattled around youth workers' meetings over such as issues as youth-versus-community, demand-led responsive work versus educational issue-based work, and volunteer involvement versus paid and qualified staff, simply 'exposed just how far this profession still was from clarifying and establishing a core and credible identity …which left those looking on—especially national and local politicians and policy makers—far from convinced by the service's claims'.

Sometimes relentless cuts in local education authority budgets further diminished and unsettled the profession through the eighties, and Davies brings the story up to date with reflections on how the current Labour government is very consciously addressing youth policy. The traditional local education authority based youth service, however, is not being prioritised as a vehicle for current government initiatives. Davies ends with the regret that 'as the 20th century closed…the inheritance both of a distinctive form of practice known as youth work and of a youth service specifically mandated to guarantee this was looking more brittle than at almost any time in its 60 year history'.

There is a possibility that this relative marginalisation of the service is at least in part the responsibility of those who have worked to establish its particular form of professionalism. There is something in the charge of 'conservatism' that Tony Blair and other politicians put in the direction of particular groups of professional workers when these groups assert their own self-identity and agendas against emerging policy priorities being developed by elected representatives. In the case of youth work, the importance of moments such as Albemarle, and the embedding of particular configurations of values into training courses and patterns of management supervision, have arguably led to a culture in which new proposals and ideas for addressing youth issues have been measured and compared against an already formed and fixed view of 'what youth work is'. Davies himself reflects that, for example, 'some of the sectarianism which characterised the service's less tolerant debates could be traced back to hardline positions in which workers were confirmed, or into which they were inducted, by their training. Their over-concentration on critical appraisal of social policy—in itself an important skill for youth workers—sometimes also encouraged knee-jerk oppositional stances to new (especially state-sponsored) initiatives, resulting in the professional service being left behind by events.'

Mike Waite

Mike Waite worked for Local Education Authority youth services in Lancashire and on the Wirral between 1986 and 1995, and was chair of the Lancashire branch of the Community and Youth Workers Union

Wales, history and identity

Chris Williams, *Capitalism, Community and Conflict: The South Wales Coalfield 1898–1947* (University of Wales Press, Cardiff, 1998), xvi+146 pp., ISBN 0-7083-1-473-2, £7.99 pbk.

Chris Williams opens his assessment of the trials and tribulations of the South Wales coalfield in the period 1898-1947 by explaining that the coalfield was 'primarily an economic phenomenon' (p.1). While the obvious overall objective of mining the rich seams of the South Wales Valleys was, of course, to enrich the mineowners, there quickly developed a series of political and cultural activities that, to a great extent, eclipsed the purely economic factors. This is not to blithely dismiss the economic poverty endured by the miners and their families but, for example, it is evident that Hywel Francis' and Dai Smith's vision of the South Wales coalfield—in their 1980 work *The Fed*—as some sort of socialist elysium is uncertain. As Williams comments, 'whether this [Francis and Smith's] characterization can be sustained in its totality is open to serious doubt' (pp.4–5). Perhaps the best guidance is to say that all the available histories of the South Wales mining communities, including Williams's own, should be read in conjunction with an 'alternative' viewpoint. Historical accounts of industrial regions tend to have a severe political slant and, although Williams generally manages to avoid polemic, when chronicling accounts of the impoverishment and deprivation encountered in the mining districts of South Wales there is, on the whole, a Byronic tendency among historians.

Williams, however, succeeds in offering a concise and absorbing account of coalfield society in the first half of the twentieth century. Starting with a detailed historiographical chapter, *Historical Perspectives*, in which a comprehensive literature guide to South Walian mining history has been assembled, *Capitalism, Community and Conflict* sets about foraying into life in the Valleys through the use of primary documentary sources, which give this publication a far more authentic feel than some other narratives that borrow from secondary references.

Chris Williams really gets to grip with his subject matter at the beginning of the second chapter. Informing us how, in the second half of the nineteenth century, 'great strides were made in the exploitation of the area's reserves of steam coal' (p.11), Williams covers a range of fascinating topics including how the wage rates for miners were double those of agricultural workers (p.11) and how, in consideration of mining, 'across the period 1901-13, Welsh workers…were five-and-a-half times more strike-prone than the

British average for all workers' (p.15). It is, however, the parallel rise of coal production and industrial militancy that resonates throughout the chapter. Despite a boom in output for the purposes of war, a strike in 1915—called by colliers who, against the instructions of their own Executive Council, felt that they should be entitled to share in the prosperity of wartime production—showed how far apart capitalist and proletariat really were. In the words of J. Vyrnwy Morgan, 'the circumstances of the war intensified the men's convictions that they were being exploited by their employers and by the Government' (p.19).

The ensuing two chapters, *The Industry and Trade Unionism*, show the aforementioned parallelism. *The Industry* commences with Williams' statement that South Wales, in the period covered by the book, was virtually a 'mono-industrial society' (p.27). The only rider that I would add to this is that while there is no doubt that coal predominated, other heavy industries, particularly steel, also played a significant part in the development of the unique politico-economic society to be found within the South Wales Valleys.

For me the most interesting chapter in the book is the one entitled *Politics*. This is because, to quote Williams, 'the south Wales coalfield provided the Labour Party with its most consistent reservoir of support across Britain as a whole' (p.49). Although this blanket support upholds the idea that 'the valleys were Labour property', one should not forget, as Williams reminds us, that, with thirty-eight branches and a membership of 2,300, 'the Communist Party tended to be the most active of all political groups in the coalfield' (p.58). Also, when considering a sociological appraisement on life in the coalfield, it is notable that Williams maintains that 'the Communist Party was more successful than Labour in providing a distinctive, separate culture' (p.58).

The *Politics* chapter captures the pivotal role that the mining communities, and the South Wales Miners Federation in particular, played in ensuring a long line of radical and socialist politicians—such as Aneurin Bevan, James Griffiths and S.O. Davies—emanated from South Wales. As Williams pronounces towards the end of the section, 'over four-fifths of coalfield MP's had been miners' (p.61). The journey from colliery to Commons was thus established and this process of 'civic embourgeoisment' remains unique in British political history.

When Williams turns his attention to a consideration of society and societal formation, he discloses how the presentation of Wales as a homogenous, organic whole conceals the truly fractured nature of coalfield life. Interestingly, the chapter entitled Society unfolds with the often-ignored issue of gender relations. Williams lays emphasis on how female socio-economic advancement in South Wales was thwarted by a combination of economic and ideological factors. As he describes, 'in 1921...only 19 per cent of the female population over twelve were regarded as occupied'.(p.63) This contrasts with the British average of 33 per cent. Furthermore, given the patriarchal setting, as far as women were concerned, 'only slowly, and against considerable hostility from organized religion and from many male politicians, was advice on birth control officially made available'.(p.66)

Overall, it is fair to say that *Capitalism, Community and Conflict* presents a worthy account of its chosen time and place. However, where the book really flourishes is in its willingness to examine lateral issues, such as gender relations and ethnic groups, which until recent decades were ignored by historians and academics alike. Allied with the extensive bibliography and segments of illustrative documents, Chris Williams has succeeded in compiling a beneficial and readily accessible text.

Alan Sandry
Centre for Public Policy, University of Wales, Swansea

Britain's different modernities

Becky Conekin, Frank Mort and Chris Waters (eds), *Moments of Modernity: Reconstructing Britain 1945–1964* (Rivers Oram Press, London, 1999) xi+290pp., ISBN 1-85489-105-7, £14.95 pbk.

This collection provides twelve accounts of the British experience in the twenty years following the end of the Second World War. Many challenge prevailing histories of the period, regarded as over-generalisations that fail to take account of the different modernities that emerged at this moment, and of the uneven pace of change across and within different sectors. As the editors note in their thorough introduction, modernity is a troubled idea, but has a particular moment of focus in Britain after the Second World War, and they intend to 'use the idea of modernity to focus a conceptual debate on the significance of this period'.(p.20)

The distinctly different moments of post war austerity and reconstruction and the later affluence of this period provides the underlying structure for many of the chapters. Peter Mandler contrasts the expert-led modernity of national planning established under the Labour Government with the modernity of the private developer-led approach to urban planning, driven by consumer sovereignty, that resulted in the many disastrous city centre redevelopments towards the end of this period. Martin Francis's analysis of the self restraint practised by leading members of the Labour Party is shown to be congruent with the period of austerity, but out of step with the emergence of affluence. Pat Thane's account of population politics, which continued pre-War anxieties about population decline, provides a vehicle to discuss the double sided nature of modernity: its tendency towards uniformity and its emphasis on individual autonomy and the desire to assert it.

The emergence of individual autonomy and new identities is the major theme of the book. The editors and a number of the contributors use the concept of the reflexive self and the development of personhood through lifestyle choices, used by Giddens to investigate late modernity, to investigate its origins in this earlier period. Carolyn Steedman uses these concepts to examine the development of creative autobiographical writing in schools during the 1950s and the apparently new valuing of the working class voice, although she also recognises a longer history of making the poor construct narratives about their lives in order to satisfy the demands of Poor Law guardians and social security offices. Chris Waters develops this theme of new and distinctive modes for imagining the self through his account of Peter Wildeblood's book *Against the Law*, written after his imprisonment under laws against homosexuality in 1955. However, Wildeblood is only able to define his own identity in the terms allowed for by the current discourses of homosexuality.

Waters also shows how opposition to emergent sexual identities was grounded in the maintenance of class distinction. At the trial, much was made of the transgression of social boundaries through the public school educated Wildeblood's choice of a younger working class Glaswegian as his sexual partner. However, compared to this example of class-rigidity, Frank Mort, writing about the growth of cultural management of demand through advertising, illustrates that by the late 1950s, leading advertisers were recognising that economic class groupings were becoming inadequate to categorise the emergent differentiated lifestyles of consumers.

The development of new identities is most thoroughly considered by Bill Schwarz who uses the figure of the white South African leader, Jan Smuts, to consider the challenges and changes to the construction of English identity. By the time of his death in 1950, Smuts was regarded as one of the greatest imperial statesman, pulled into the force-field of English ethnicity, and reviving it as no domestic could. However, plans to erect a statue to Smuts in Parliament Square were troubled by the inappropriateness of his politics to the new focus on decolonisation. The statue was finally erected in 1956, coinciding exactly with the unmasking of Britain's imperial pretensions at the Suez Canal, but it was a feeble event, minimally reported and celebrated. Schwarz argues that Smuts had 'slipped out of the defining rhythms of popular memory', although his legacy of a politics of race, providing a notion of what it was to be white, continued to be used by sections of the British population wishing to assert that Britain was 'a white man's country' as earlier notions of imperialism and the primal colonial encounter were relocated into the domestic domain.

Schwarz's paper, which with Frank Mort's is the most theoretically wide-ranging, raises a problem current throughout the book. Whilst its subtitle is 'Reconstructing Britain 1945–1964', the focus tends to be on England, and the construction of a new English identity. Thus, Martin Francis notes how in the context of the Labour Party's emphasis on restraint and emotional control, the 'vermin' speech of Nye Bevan in 1948 was excused by some because he was Welsh.

A related theme is a critique of the thesis of the Americanisation of British culture during this period. Mort uses the success of the menswear retailer Burtons to indicate how, although it was dedicated to mass retailing, it avoided American models of mass advertising and maintained local strategies for advertising and marketing, focusing on the shop window, and using forms of aristocratic symbolism around the 'gentleman'. Similarly, Nick Tiratsoo illustrates how US Technical Assistance programmes established in 1948 to aid European industry, were indifferently received by British managers. In a different vein, Peter Bailey provides an autobiographical account of being an America-obsessed, jazz playing adolescent in Coventry in the early 1950s, and argues that his experience of modernity was of a conservative and distinctly English type, in which fantasies of hyper-modern America were contained within welfarism and a self-regarding national culture.

These papers were initially written before 'New Labour' came to power and do not comment on similarities with the modernisation themes of the current Government or, in Becky Conekin's final chapter on the Festival of Britain, with the Dome and other Millennium extravagances. As a sociologist and not a historian, it is impossible to comment on the significance of these papers to post-war historiography. However, as someone who has lived through all but three years of this period, I found the similarities and the differences with the present thought provoking and stimulating, not least as a challenge to monolithic postmodernist accounts.

Roger Woods
University of Luton

Laura Marcus and Lynda Nead (eds), *The Actuality of Walter Benjamin* (Lawrence and Wishart in association with *New Formations*, London, 1998), 224pp., ISBN 0-85315-863-0, £13.99 pbk.

Commemoration seems too bland a word to describe the way we return to the works of Bertolt Brecht and Walter Benjamin. We need a vocabulary closer to Benjamin's explorations of the potential 'electrical contact' between past and present, and the 'white-hot topicality' he urged on the historian. In October last year, for example, Lothar Bisky, Chair of the German Party of Democratic Socialism, spoke at a 'matinée' to mark the 50th anniversary of the founding of the GDR. Part of this event took place in the Berliner Ensemble, and Bisky wound up his recollection of the GDR years on a self-critical note, with two Brechtian comments:

> [It was] a fundamental error to believe that it could be meaningful and necessary to avoid discussion, criticism and arguments at any price. That's why Brecht never wrote his Rosa Luxemburg play which we might have needed so urgently, telling his biographer, Ernst Schumacher in 1952, 'I never got past the prologue…I talked it over with others. We arrived at the conclusion that a truthful treatment would only deepen the conflict with the working class movement and re-open old wounds. In the face of reaction, of the necessity to strengthen our own ranks, this would have been irresponsible'. But that's exactly what we should have done, more often and more consistently.

Bisky went on to ask what we should learn from the past: 'One of the "most important lessons" Brecht claimed to have learnt in his political life was that "a future for humankind is visible only from the bottom, from the perspective of the oppressed and the exploited. Only fighting with them one fights for humankind".'

Another illuminating return occurs in the New Year edition of *New Left Review*, which publishes the posthumous essay of Michael Sprinker on Benjamin, 'Grand Hotel Abyss'. Sprinker's passionate attempt to put together an anarchist Benjamin for our collective memory is a little too millennarian for my taste, but we might expect a surge in such readings, whether political or theological; and one by-product is a tantalising and persuasive invitation to revisit Benjamin's response to Rosa Luxemburg.

Nevertheless, there is nothing easy about celebrating these thinkers. Most of the material in the collection of essays *The Actuality of Walter Benjamin* was delivered at a centenary conference, 'Walter Benjamin 1892-1940' held at Birkbeck College, London in 1992. Irving Wolfarth, professor of German at the University of Reims, more alert to the ironies of such a venture than most of his co-participants, kicked off his robust contribution with a series of appropriately humbling Benjamin quotes:

We have, in effect to face the fact that the bourgeois apparatus of production and publication can assimilate and even propagate astonishing quantities of revolutionary themes without thereby seriously putting in question its own existence, and that of the class which owns it. This remains the case at least as long as it is routinely supplied by hacks, even revolutionary ones.

Celebration…aims to smooth over the revolutionary moments of the historical process. Its concern is to construct a continuity. It accentuates only those elements of a work which have already entered posterity. What it misses are the jagged edges which offer a foothold to someone who wants to get beyond that work.

Something from the past must be saved not so much from the contempt or disregard into which it has fallen, as from the particular way in which it has been handed down. The way in which it is celebrated as our 'heritage' is more ominous than any oblivion.

How, Wolfarth asked himself and his colleagues, 'the assembled suppliers', could they avoid the fate of the revolutionary hack 'serving up a culinary Benjamin to the jaws of the culture industry'? Was it possible, in fact, to 'imagine an international Benjamin conference which…made a difference?'

Elsewhere in the volume, Julian Roberts, professor of philosophy at the University of Munich, claims that this act of self-flagellation at the entry-post to Benjamin commentary has become a familiar feature of the 'lamentational mode' much in evidence in the 'world-wide scholarly industry' which now surrounds him. Roberts's concern is to rescue the most comprehensive and penetrating aesthetic theorist of the last century from such 'apocalyptic' moralising. But he concedes that Benjamin's own considerable failure as an academic 'gives the brew particular spice'.

In Roberts's full-length account (Macmillan, 1982) of Benjamin's emergence as the leading theorist of revolutionary cultural organisation, we are introduced rather early to Benjamin's contempt for the weakness of intellectuals. Their failure in making any significant contribution to the collective solidarity which alone stands between Europe and war or later, fascism, is a constant theoretical and practical preoccupation. In 1914, the youthful Benjamin's disgust is directed at the mobilisation of professorial support behind what he saw as the dismal illusion of the German 'national interest'. In the mid 1920s, he is writing letters back from Moscow, asking, 'But for whom are we writing? Do you know the answer?'. And the same issue is central to his historic relationships with Brecht and the Frankfurt School a decade later.

Throughout, his attitude to academics remained dismissive. Academics, as Roberts puts it in the later essay, are 'precisely that part of the intellectual world defined by their having been officially coopted by the other side'.

Given this, it is tempting to see more than a streak of masochism in the world-wide Benjamin industry, which shows no sign of diminishing as we enter the new millennium. Alex Honneth, a professor at the Institute of Philosophy in Frankfurt/Main, does not go quite this far, but the opening of his interesting study of the relationship between anthropology and philosophy of history in Benjamin's works is a sustained, even irritated meditation on what we might call, the Benjamin challenge.

'Scarcely any other [twentieth century] author', he suggests, 'has been able to trigger so many waves of reception in so short a time'. To the advocates of Critical Theory, of Marxism, of Jewish mysticism, all competing for an appropriate understanding, we may now add the proponents of deconstruction, post-modernism, and even supporters of a conservative theory of politics. Everybody wants to have a piece of Benjamin. An enormous amount of interpretative work has been done. Yet in Honneth's view, this ever-increasing group of scholars have between them yielded no significant theoretical fruits in philosophy, the theory of culture, social research, or scientific debate: 'his theory has no recognisable effect'.

The problem, he argues, is the difficulty of bringing together Benjamin's 'scattered, frequently disparate ideas…in themselves of surprising stringency, indeed of alluring brilliance' into 'larger complexes which could enter…discourse on a competitive basis'. This is no accident, Honneth suspects. Benjamin's ideas 'intentionally lack' such unity. His writings 'resist every kind of theory formation'. As a result, he accuses Benjamin of being 'contemporaneous today…only in the most trivial sense.'

A similar, if rather more temperamental, tone of reproach enters into Janet Wolff's thoughts on why Benjamin is 'not a great help' to feminist and post-colonial cultural studies. Wolff ventures to accuse Benjamin of 'colluding with a patriarchal construction of modernity', because the Baudelairean flaneur he identifies as a central figure epitomising modern urban experience, has no female equivalent, 'since women weren't (and for that matter, aren't) at liberty to engage in aimless and anonymous strolling.' Her overall concern is whether Benjamin is really matching up to developments in contemporary academe. He scores well with the burgeoning theorists of 'urban space' in 1992—although she is not sure how to bring together two winning lines in 'cities' and 'exile'—but less well in his rather 'exclusive' thinking in images, from a feminist perspective.

For a non-academic scanning the field in this anthology, what is so inescapable is the strength of the Benjaminian response to such concerns. Only turn from Honneth to Wohlfarth's few choice and incandescent quotes, and it is clear that Benjamin's 'jagged edges which offer a foothold to someone who wants to get beyond that work' are precisely designed to pierce beneath the smooth surface, to tease and defy a commodity fetishism reducing all thought to competing 'large complexes' in the academic market. Wolff's business-like charting of the 'convergence of certain contemporary concerns' with 'central aspects of Benjamin's oeuvre' based on a list of the 'particular investments' currently belonging to some academic disciplines, takes us back to the stark choice for modern writers Benjamin analysed in his first Baudelaire essay. As Roberts puts it, rather succinctly: 'contract on the terms of the market, or starve'.

Benjamin's insistent question is to ask which struggles are worth engaging in, under these conditions. It is not at all clear, for example, what use is really served by the two essays sporting urban space theory in this anthology, beyond the immediate 'investments' of a relatively new arrival in the 'scholarly industry'. How quickly 'the contemporaneous' dates, compared to those illuminating Benjamin quotes—which time and again throw the ball back into the court of his commentators!

To say this is not at all to argue that Benjamin is always right. It might indeed be easier to defend the thesis that he was a rather spectacular historical loser. Indeed, Wohlfarth has a strong and thought-provoking formulation of this question—why the interest?—in relation to the elusive 'Theses on the Philosophy of History', written just prior to Benjamin's suicide, as a response to the Nazi-Soviet pact of August 1939. He outlines three facts which must weigh heavily on any present-day reading, and which take us immediately to the centre of the struggles for survival that Benjamin did think it worth engaging in:

> First, it was not the theologico-political strategy proposed in the first Thesis that won the war against Fascism; the 'allied victory' was a quite different, much messier, more mixed affair. Second, we now know that the attempt to bring about a revolutionary state of emergency under postrevolutionary conditions led, when literally acted out, to the dead end of urban terrorism. Thirdly, the political system that has, mercifully outlasted Fascist and Communist totalitarianisms is also the one which.. represents the opposite, indeed the betrayal of everything Benjamin stood for. The future lies for the time being with social democracy...

Why, in short, should we interest ourselves in an intellectual who got so much wrong? From the evidence in this anthology, we can make a provisional answer. It is something to do with the fact that he is so serious a thinker. Those essays which take the time to investigate his theoretical and political concerns, acting as a midwife for the reader and delivering access to some of the vast continents of knowledge which he explored, show how 'stringent' indeed are the questions he formulated as worthwhile answering. The more generous the intellectual sharing of this heritage, the closer these essayists come to the central Benjaminian injunction to revolutionise the relations of knowledge production and distribution. And there is a lot of generosity in this volume.

Roberts patiently takes us through the history of aesthetics after Kant, and gives us a glimpse of what Benjamin's theory of conflict brings to his constantly alluring and brilliant criticism. Honneth's own explorations of Benjamin's response to Ernst Junger's anthropological materialism via Proust, Bergson and Klages yield fascinating insights into his theory of redemptive history. This in turn, opens the door to further continents in Gillian Rose's impressive and moving excavations into modern Judaist thinking, and the social justice required by the existence of poverty, pain and suffering.

In the end, what matters is not whether we succeed in pulling Benjamin into the historical materialist camp; the 'ultra-leftist' camp of Michael Sprinker's posthumous essay; or the theological camp. Roberts comes as near to achieving the first as anyone could realistically expect, only to find himself wondering three pages from the end of his study whether Benjamin was ever more than a 'Heideggerian in left-wing clothes who…finally re-entered the fold when it became clear that Bolshevism had failed'.

What matters far more, is to see how the Jewish belief in a deferred redemption which is promised, not to the individual, but to the whole of society and the whole of history, fills out the messianic elements of the Marxist quest for a meaningful life in Benjamin's intellectual struggle, and in return, makes political activity and organisation the potential bearer of the highest ethical and spiritual aspirations. Where would we place the conceptual shoe-horn, for example, between the theological and Marxist overtones in Brecht's 'important lesson', as quoted by Bisky above, that we can only envision the future of humankind from the vantage point of the oppressed?

Does it matter if Benjamin was for or against certain forms of social democracy? No. But it does matter that he warned us about the complacency built into assumptions of historical progress; that the search for the modern is not enough; that more is required than political or organisational advance—that if we are to fend off the horrors of warfare and the destruction of civilisations, experience itself must be transformed.

Martin Jay writes that the obscure concept of 'experience...has rightly been called Benjamin's great theme', and gives us a useful brief account of the context for Benjamin's evolving theory. He goes on, rather disappointingly, to look at style indirect libre in the novel form. More usefully, he could have explored the 'double translation' effect of Benjaminian literary criticism as an example of how the electric flash between past and present can illuminate and transform our experience. Alternatively, he could have returned to Benjamin's mature interest in and commitment to Brechtian practice. The neglect of this, the most fecund stage of Benjamin's deliberations as an avant-garde intellectual searching for the right professional context, seems strange in a book entitled *The Actuality of Walter Benjamin*.

However, as a recent editor of *New Times* magazine who has played a part in consolidating the social democratic aspirations of what is now being called the *New Politics Network* (formerly *Democratic Left*), I am more than ever grateful for another volume which brings me such glorious quotes as this one from Benjamin's last work *On the Concept of History*, in which he insists that history itself must be brushed against its grain, if we are to find what is revolutionary, as we must, in unrevolutionary times:

> We know that the Jews were prohibited from investigating the future. *The Torah* and the prayers instruct them in remembrance, however. This stripped the future of its magic, to which all those succumb who turn to the sooth-sayers for enlightenment. Yet this does not imply that for the Jews the future turned into homogeneous, empty time. For every second of time was the straight gate through which the Messiah might enter.

Rosemary Bechler
Rosemary Bechler edited the former magazine New Times

Globalisation, the longer view

Willie Thompson, *Global Expansion: Britain and its Empire, 1870–1914* (London: Pluto Press, 1999), 160pp., ISBN 0-74531-235-7, £9.99 pbk.

Thompson has called his book *Global Expansion* because that is the context in which he argues that British imperial expansion during the period from 1870 to 1914 must be viewed. After all, Britain's late nineteenth-century drive for colonies can only be understood in terms of the parallel activities of other imperial states forming part of the global system during this stage of development.

Thompson suggests a framework for analysis, a modified form of Giovanni

Arrighi's 'regimes of accumulation'. According to this framework, from the fifteenth century onward, the global economy passed through several regimes of accumulation, or stages of development that resulted in the expansion, consolidation, and institutionalisation of world capital. During each phase, one particular state commanded the central economy, and the owners of capital in that state were thereby able to dominate the circuits of global exchange in whatever form they took at the time. Consequently, each regime of accumulation was characterised by competition among the major powers to gain ascendancy and control over the global economic system. However, the shift from one regime of accumulation to another was determined by fundamental changes in the forces of production—so that the second regime of accumulation was characterised by slave labour, the third by machine production, and the fourth by steam, chemical and electric power sources.

By viewing British imperial expansion in the context of general European endeavours in the same direction, Thompson is able to show not only that the 1870s marked a significant shift in global politics, but also how the First World War came about. He argues that Britain, which presided over the previous regime of accumulation, began to lose its dominant position during the fourth regime because it failed to adapt to the economic values and parameters of the new era. Whereas other imperialist powers adopted a protectionist stance in an effort to match British industrial growth, Britain retained its 'imperialism of free trade' ethos, and so was forced to accumulate a massive formal empire to preserve open spheres of trade—even though it would have preferred less costly informal relationships. As a consequence, rival powers were able to overtake Britain in its markets, whereas it could not gain entry to theirs. Moreover, while other countries (such as the US) were net importers of capital or (as in Germany) benefited from state subsidies and the production of finance capital, Britain continued to be a major exporter of investment capital and neglected to channel funds into improving and expanding its home industries. Naturally its relative industrial performance suffered, and rival powers quickly closed the gap to Britain's position of industrial dominance. When, in the early part of the twentieth century, Germany issued a leadership challenge, Britain's only available response was to form alliances with France and Russia. This helps to explain how military blocs formed around the two rival claimants to global hegemony—a situation that culminated in world war in 1914.

The regimes of accumulation framework allows Thompson to critically assess Lenin's theory of imperialism, since the First World War is seen as a competitive struggle between rival powers to dominate that or the next regime of accumulation. As Thompson put it: 'The bloody contest which got underway in 1914 was therefore not so much, as Lenin phrased it, a struggle for the redivision of the world as one to determine who its leading commercial power should be; compared to which the redistribution of colonial real estate or even spheres of trade and investment opportunity were important but secondary concerns.' (p. 93). He is also able to provide a boost to Hobson's claim that British expansionism was detrimental to Britain's economy, by diverting capital abroad rather than using it to improve and expand British industry.

While Thompson's general premise is a good one, the book's structure does not allow his argument to shine forth. The text is organised chronologically rather than conceptually, which means that the reader runs the risk of forgetting that the book is operating within the analytical framework of regimes of accumulation (and Thompson fails to provide periodic focal points to direct the reader's attention to this). The argument further falters from Thompson's choices of section headings, which often do not convey either what material is being covered or the importance of the evidence being presented. More problematic is that the same material is frequently repeated throughout the text, which causes one to wonder whether the book could have been shortened. These criticisms are directed as much at the publisher as the author.

One final point that the reader should bear in mind: this book does not contain any new research or theoretical perspective. However, this is not a criticism. After all, Thompson freely admits that his book is 'primarily a descriptive account of one particular imperialism' (Preface, p.ix). Thompson's main contribution here is to provide a useful framework that generates an alternative interpretation of known historical events, rather than uncovering new facts. And while Thompson tends to over rely on two sources—that is, Cain and Hopkin's British Imperialism: Innovation and Expansion and Stockwell's edited *Cambridge Illustrated History of the British Empire*—his work represents an important contribution to the literature on empire and theories of imperialism.

Thompson's book would be extremely useful for readers wishing to learn more about British imperial relations on a global basis, with regard to both Britain's formal and informal dependencies. It provides a framework for analysing, not only the period from 1870 to 1914, but also much of British history up to the present. Moreover, because Thompson deals with the British imperial state system as a whole and places it within the context of the global system of states and the productive forces characteristic of the time, his framework may be used to gain an understanding of other areas of the world.

Gita Subrahmanyam
Gita Subrahmanyam is a lecturer in politics at Birkbeck College, London

Correspondence

Narrating the Thirties

I read Roger Spalding's purported critique of our book *Narrating the Thirties* (*Socialist History 14*, pp.54–67), with a growing feeling that it was really about something else. Readers must judge for themselves the validity of his criticisms, but they should be warned that the book is not, as they may be expecting, a study of British politics in the Second World War, but of the formation and uses of historical memory, in this case memory of the 1930s. One chapter discusses wartime constructions of the 1930s. Twelve pages of this chapter form the sole object of this thirteen-page critique (a ratio which I find rather flattering—is it, I wonder, some kind of record?). The remaining seven chapters and 200-odd pages—including the alleged postmodernist tendencies provocatively highlighted by your editorial trailer—do not get a look-in. I think Spalding really wants to write about the war: perhaps he should do so, and leave our book to those who are prepared to engage with its arguments.

It is not good practice to take issue with one's reviewers, but I am obliged to do so because Spalding misrepresents our book on a number of points. We do not, as he suggests, ignore the cinema: film is dealt with prominently in four of our seven chapters—though not in the war chapter, since space is limited, and wartime films have been well picked over by other scholars. Most of the films Spalding discusses do not deal with the 1930s and therefore are not relevant to our argument, though they may be relevant to some other debate. We never argued that 'Churchillians' 'did not address the prewar past', though we could, I agree, have said more about the ways that they did: however, what Spalding says on the subject does not (as he seems to think) contradict our argument, which is that left and right had different views of the 1930s, and that these played a more prominent part in the rhetoric of the left. Nor do we claim that wartime pamphlets like *Guilty Men* (1940) and

Your MP (1944) 'actually reshaped popular consciousness'. This would, as he says, be 'a very large claim to make'. However, we do not make it.

Finally, and rather more seriously, Spalding accuses us of sharp practice over a quote from J. B. Priestley on pp.135-6 of *Narrating the Thirties*. We omit part of the quoted passage, and signal this in the conventional way, with three dots: I think it's called 'ellipsis'. In Spalding's quotation from the book, the three dots are left out, making it look as if we were not just omitting the words, but deliberately suppressing their existence. This is, I am sure, a mistake: however, in view of the imputation of intellectual underhandedness which this evidence is used to support, it is a singularly unfortunate mistake. If Spalding was a cop, I'd say I'd been fitted up.

Readers who want to know what we really said in *Narrating the Thirties* are advised to consult the book itself: still in print, and a rattling good read. Those, however, who agree with Roger Spalding, that all views of the 1930s (such as Will Hutton's) which contradict his own received opinions are by definition so wrong that they don't even deserve to be refuted, will find little comfort there. As for the Second World War, I look forward to reading more of Spalding's views on the subject: I expect I will disagree with them, but that's another matter.

John Baxendale
(co-author with Chris Pawling of *Narrating the Thirties*, Basingstoke, 1996)
Sheffield Hallam University

Roger Spalding replies:

My piece on *Narrating the Thirties* did not purport to be a review of the whole book. My opening paragraph outlined the central themes of the book before going on to focus on a specific issue—the construction of a particular view of the 1930s created during the Second World War. This seemed a perfectly justifiable approach because, no matter how much space Baxendale and Pawling gave over to the war, the experience of that war was a central element within their argument. As a consequence of that experience, it is claimed, a narrative of the 1930s emerged that predominated in British society until 1979.

Baxendale argues that the films I mention 'do not deal with the 1930s'. This is not quite the case, what he really means is that they are not set in the 1930s. The majority of wartime war films present a view of the war in which the upper-middle classes are firmly in control. Such people did not spring full-grown from the ground in September 1939, they were, of course, the product of the society of the 1930s. Consequently films which present such figures as natural war leaders directly validate the class structure of the 1930s.

Baxendale denies that he claims that the wartime Gollancz pamphlets 're-shaped popular consciousness'. What he actually says is:

> The dominance of these negative views of the Thirties thus both reflected and helped to constitute the ideological ascendancy of the centre-Left during the 1940s.

Helping to constitute an ideological ascendancy sounds like re-shaping popular consciousness to me.

Baxendale claims that I misrepresent them by claiming that they said the 'Churchillians' did not address the immediate pre-war past. However, they do state:

> Thus, while the Churchillian narrative is hardly a narrative at all—rather, a single, continuous state of national being, punctuated by dramatic incidents illustrating what is always true about the British nation—the People's War offered a shorter, more urgent narrative of past, present and future, focussing crucially on the Thirties...

A clear distinction is being drawn here between the left who foregrounded the 1930s and the Churchillians who did not. The point of quoting Conservative views of the 1930s was not, as Baxendale implies, simply to demonstrate that their views were different from those of the left, but to demonstrate that a number of Conservatives incorporated a view of the 1930s into a broad historical narrative.

A key element of my argument against Baxendale and Pawling is that the distinctions they draw between left and right were not as clear as they claim. The left was just as likely to appeal to ancient historical traditions as the right. This brings us to J.B. Priestley. According to Baxendale I accuse him and his co-author of 'sharp practice' in their use of a Priestley quotation. What I actually said was that Baxendale and Pawling 'greatly strengthen their case by their editing of this passage'. Unfortunately the three dots indicating an ellipsis were left out of the quoted passage in my article. This was my mistake, and I apologise for it. However, by this ellipsis the quotation is shaped to fit their People's War mould, demonstrating a narrative 'focussing crucially on the Thirties'. The sentences removed, however, have a positively Churchillian tone, focussing as they do on the glories of the England of Constable and Cotman. Baxendale and Pawling have simply dumped those elements of Priestley that do not fit their argument. If I were a cop I should think I had them bang to rights on this.

Narrating the Thirties is an interesting book, and is one I recommend to my own students. It is not, though, whatever John Baxendale may think, without flaws.

Labour's Africa

Paul Kelemen's article 'Labour's Africa and the Mau Mau Rebellion' (*Socialist History* 17, pp.43–60) gives inadequate coverage to the support within the Labour Party and on the left in general for the cause of freedom in Kenya—and Africa as a whole.

Although he mentions a speech by Fenner Brockway, emphasising that land hunger was Mau Mau's immediate cause, he fails to deal with the work of the Congress of Peoples Against Imperialism (formed 1948) or the Movement for Colonial Freedom (MCF, formed 1954), with which Fenner Brockway was closely associated. Both organisations played a significant role in mobilising opinion in favour of the colonial revolution which, in due course, became dominant among Labour Party activists.

Fenner Brockway, who first visited Kenya in 1950 and outraged settler opinion by staying with Africans, returned with his fellow Labour MP, Leslie Hale, in 1952, after the Mau Mau crisis had begun. They supported the demands of the Kenya Africa Union for full self-government, opposed the arrests of seven of its leaders, including Jomo Kenyatta, and tried to get the support of all groups represented in the Legislative Assembly for African rights. Unfortunately, the European members withdrew their signatures, following Mau Mau threats against Michael Blundell, the settlers' leader.

In Britain, Joseph Murumbi, Secretary of the banned Kenya Africa Union, addressed meetings, despite official Labour Party attempts to prevent this, and I personally remember participating in one in Newcastle-under-Lyme in 1953. Later, Murumbi became Secretary of the MCF for a period—a fact which illustrates the strength of its commitment on Kenya.

The MCF provided Parliamentary Questions and briefings for sponsor MPs, published leaflets and pamphlets and organised meetings and demonstrations on all colonial issues, including Kenya. Barbara Castle was particularly outspoken, and denounced in the House of Commons the beating to death of eleven African prisoners at Hola Camp in Kenya.

The fact that Jim Griffiths, the Labour Party spokesman, demanded action on the land problem, against the colour bar, for increases in wages, the extension of free education and democratisation of local government, reflected the pressure of opinion in the Party.

To argue that 'Labour disagreed…with the means which the Conservative

Government employed to defeat Mau Mau rather than with its over all political objectives' (p.55) does less than justice to the campaign within the Labour Party completely to end colonial rule. In this campaign, the role played by the MCF was by no means without importance, but it embraced many who were not MCF members.

The view that dissociation from Mau Mau terrorism—often directed at Africans, anyway—(or, for that matter, rejection of Kenyatta's support for female circumcision) demonstrates that the Labour Party as a whole was half-hearted about decolonialisation, overlooks the profound commitment of a large section of the party to full freedom and to continuing opposition to undemocratic cliques and exploitation by multinational corporations.

Stan Newens
President, Liberation (formerly the Movement for Colonial Freedom)

Paul Kelemen replies:

I focused in my article on the Labour Party leadership's approach to Kenya and mainly from the 1930s to the outbreak of the Mau Mau rebellion, in the early 1950s. I touched on the anti-colonial, humanitarian tradition in the party, articulated by African specialists such as Norman Leys, and briefly referred to the constituency parties' demand for the leadership to condemn the military repression during the Kenyan emergency. I was principally concerned, however, with the ideas generated by the Fabian Colonial Bureau which from 1940—forming part of a broader, modernising perspective within the political establishment—which was the main source of ideas for the party leadership's view on colonial matters. I fast-forwarded the discussion at the end of the article to cover the leadership's position up to the 1960-61 independence negotiations and, for this period, I was wrong not to refer to the role of the Movement for Colonial Freedom. This omission does not affect, however, my account of the dominant position in the party.

The MCF, formed in 1954 to support independence struggles in the colonies, became, as Stan Newens points out, a significant influence within the labour movement. But the party leadership did its utmost to keep the MCF at arm's length and at one point tried to set up a rival, more compliant, organisation. In November 1956, the Secretary to the Labour Party's Commonwealth Sub-Committee, referring to a resolution calling for the NEC to give active support to the MCF, commented: 'As the latter is a non-party body, which includes among its membership the members of other British political party [sic], and as at its last year's Annual Conference it passed a resolution directly contrary to party policy, such support seems undesirable.'[1] The TUC General Council was equally hostile to MCF activities. It declared that the TUC had 'established its own channels for co-operation with colonial unions' and 'does not approve of the intervention of the Movement of Colonial Freedom in the trade union field' (TUC Report, 1957). The following year, when the MCF called for British trade unions to give backing to the founding congress of an All-African Trades Union Federation, the TUC's head office referred unions to its 1957 policy statement to pressurise them into withholding their support. The TUC General Council's 'own channels for co-operation' in the colonies were based on collaborating with the Colonial Office and, from 1954 onwards, also with the Federation of Overseas Employers, to foster 'responsible' trade unions.

As I mentioned in the article, in the case of Kenya, pressure from the left of the Labour movement made party leaders increasingly critical of the Tory government's repressive policies. Stan Newens recalls above that Barbara Castle was prominent in exposing the brutal treatment of Kenyan prisoners detained in the Hola camp. He will surely also remember that, at the 1957 party conference, the motion that he seconded, which called for a future Labour government to greatly increase aid to the colonies and to transfer to their peoples the large, overseas operations of British companies, was opposed by Barbara Castle on behalf of the National Executive. The motion was defeated. The humanitarian condemnation of the brutalities of colonialism was, after 1945, generally enjoined in the Labour party with defending the economic relations that underpinned colonialism.

For the party leadership, criticism of the methods of military repression—however sincere—was also convenient for claiming to uphold the party's anti-colonial tradition and thereby stave off criticism from the left. Yet the bi-partisan approach between the two main parties remained largely intact. In 1957, the Labour leadership endorsed the Conservative government's response to the nationalist demand that the settlers' power be dismantled. It gave backing to the Lennox-Boyd constitutional proposals, which increased African representation in the Kenyan Legislative Council but retained overall control in the hands of the whites. *The Economist* (16 November 1957) noted that the underlying intention of the proposals was 'to divert the direction of constitutional development away from the "one man one vote principle", which would ensure that eventually a wholly African government would rule'. In fact, it is unlikely that by this stage even Lennox-Boyd envisaged the European settlers permanently holding onto power. He, like the Labour leadership, merely wanted to prolong the handover process until an African leadership was acceptable to the settlers.

Notwithstanding their different perspectives the Conservatives saw the settlers primarily as 'kith and kin'; Labour mainly as the key to the development of Kenyan agriculture—the two parties were yoked together by the priority they accorded to pacifying the settlers. Tom Mboya, the Kenyan nationalist and trade union leader, wrote to the Fabian Colonial Bureau: 'I regret that the party has decided to support Lennox-Boyd thus leaving us to fight it on our own. We shall, however, continue to struggle since we know that our future lies in this. The party's position has greatly influenced settler opinion to extremism.'[2]

I agree with Stan Newens that the reaction to the Mau Mau rebellion, is an inadequate yardstick by which to measure Labour's commitment to anti-colonialism (though there was more to Mau Mau than terrorism). The significance of the attitudes to this rebellion, by Labour and by other political forces, lies elsewhere. They reveal some of the assumptions of the time about Africa, about the impact of colonial rule and about which class of Africans should take over the mantle of leadership in preparation for independence.

The argument I tried to develop in relation to the Labour leadership's colonial policy was that it provided ideological support for, and helped to prepare, a neo-colonial solution in Kenya. This clearly does not apply to the MCF, but the latter was nevertheless largely uncritical of the neo-colonial structures which were put in place with Kenyatta's accession to power. The final land settlement negotiated at Lancaster House, while providing generous compensation to departing European farmers, left many Africans landless and the Kenyan economy in the grip of international capital. This is not to deny, though, the MCF's role in raising awareness about imperialism from which later campaigns in solidarity with struggles in Vietnam, Ireland, Oman, Palestine, South Africa, Nicaragua, Eritrea etc. were also able to benefit.

Notes

1. Labour Party Commonwealth Sub-Committee, minutes, agenda, documents, file 1956–57, Labour Party Archives, National Museum of Labour History, Manchester.
2. Mboya to Betts, 1 April 1958, Fabian Colonial Bureau papers, Rhodes House, Oxford, box 115, file 1.